A-frame

CHAD RANDL

PRINCETON ARCHITECTURAL PRESS, NEW YORK

PUBLISHED BY
PRINCETON ARCHITECTURAL PRESS
37 EAST SEVENTH STREET
NEW YORK, NEW YORK 10003

For a free catalog of books, call
1.800.722.6657.
Visit our web site at www.papress.com.

This book has been supported by a
grant from the Graham Foundation for
Advanced Studies in the Fine Arts.

Editing: Jennifer N. Thompson
Design: Deb Wood

Special thanks to: Nettie Aljian, Nicola
Bednarek, Janet Behning, Megan Carey,
Penny (Yuen Pik) Chu, Russell
Fernandez, Jan Haux, Clare Jacobson,
John King, Mark Lamster, Nancy
Eklund Later, Linda Lee, Katharine
Myers, Jane Sheinman, Scott Tennent,
and Joseph Weston of Princeton
Architectural Press —Kevin C. Lippert,
publisher

Library of Congress
Cataloging-in-Publication Data

Randl, Chad.
  A-frame / Chad Randl.
    p. cm.
Includes bibliographical references and
index.
  ISBN 1-56898-410-3 (pbk. : alk. paper)
  1. Vacation homes—United States.
  2. A-frame houses—United States.
  3. Architecture—United States—20th
century. I. Title.
  NA7575.R35 2004
  728.7'2'0973—dc22

                              2003024853

PAGE 21: From *The Complete Tales of Winnie-the-Pooh*
by A. A. Milne, illustrated by E. H. Shepard. This pres-
entation copyright © 1994 by Dutton Children's Books.
Coloring of the illustration copyright © 1992 by Dutton
Children's Books. *The House at Pooh Corner* by A. A.
Milne, illustrated by E. H. Shepard, copyright © 1928
by E. P Dutton & Co., Inc., copyright renewal 1956 by
A. A. Milne. Used by permission of Dutton Children's
Books, a division of Penguin Young Readers Group, a
member of Penguin Group (USA) Inc., 345 Hudson St.,
New York, NY 10014. All Rights Reserved.

ACKNOWLEDGMENTS
I would like to express my sincere gratitude to all
those who helped make this book possible. A long
list of friends, relatives, colleagues, and A-frame
enthusiasts passed along old brochures and articles, archival sources, photographs, tips on where
to find A-frames, and anecdotes about their own
experiences with triangular structures. Special
thanks are due to the designers, owners, and others connected with postwar A-frames who shared
their memories, personal photos, scrapbooks, and
in several cases, hospitality, namely, Henrik Bull,
Dr. David and Connie Hellyer, Andrew Geller, Wally
Reemelin, Bart Jacob, Sir Walter Lindal, David
Perlman, Hugh Dobson, John Seaver, and Jack
Merry. This book grew from a graduate thesis at
Cornell University; my advisors, Michael Tomlan
and Mary Woods, were ideal mentors who helped
broaden my research and focus my analysis. Alan
Hess, Jamie Jacobs, Meredith Clausen, Peggy
Smith, and Gregory Donofrio read all or portions of
the manuscript and provided thoughtful comments
and suggestions. Jakob Clausen, Gun Schönbeck,
Henrik Bull, Elena Hazelwood, Mary Loizzi, Göran
Andersson, and Björn Edlund provided transla-
tions. Jennifer Thompson was a dedicated,
patient, and encouraging editor and Deb Wood
assembled my pile of images and text into a compelling design. The Graham Foundation for
Advanced Studies in Fine Arts provided essential
support for the research and production of this
book. Final thanks go to my parents for their years
of unquestioning support and to Melissa and the
girls who are everything.

TO MELISSA, LUCY, ELLA, AND LANEY

Contents

David Perlman's A-frame, 1958

The A-Frame: An Introduction

CHAD RANDL

Stepping inside the house was like stepping back in time, with the same can opener on the kitchen wall, the same wicker chair near the window, and the same cow skin rug spread out by the fireplace. Everything matched photographs from forty-six years ago, when *Sunset* magazine put David Perlman's Squaw Valley A-frame on the cover. With so much of the past still present, it was easy to imagine the moments that had passed beneath the steeply pitched roof: Friday nights unloading the car after driving from the city, après ski parties, hot cocoas, games of Parcheesi and chess, skis piled up in the corners, and wool socks drying on the loft rail.

The owner, David Perlman, had arranged for me to pick up the keys from the local realty office while I was visiting the area. He had recently sold the house and was days away from a final trip out from San Francisco to pack up some personal belongings and say good-bye. Perlman's was not the first A-frame vacation home built after the war, but it was one of the most successful designs, balancing the visual drama of the triangular form with the functional requirements of a home away from home. And it was my favorite.

The house was built in the summer of 1955. A science writer for the *San Francisco Chronicle*, Perlman had wanted a vacation home for his family that would be close to the newly carved ski runs of Squaw Valley. Architect George Rockrise came up with a design that used intersecting gables and a T-shaped floor plan to provide a dynamic triangular exterior and a spacious, light-filled interior. With barn-like board and batten siding and a cedar-shingled roof, matching the mountain peaks above, the house was well-suited to its natural surroundings. By using a glass-walled gable end that opened onto an expansive deck, Rockrise thinned the line between inside and outside, giving the house an openness and informality that suited its function.

It was easy to see why the Perlmans loved the house (*Sunset* said it fit them like a good ski boot). Different from their year-round house in

San Francisco, it was a multifaceted design reflecting the informality and fun of a vacation while accommodating the practical needs of an active family with frequent visitors. It was modern and traditional, dramatic and economical. These attributes, shared by the few triangle vacation homes that came before and the tens of thousands that followed, helped make the A-frame the quintessential postwar vacation retreat.

The A-frame was the right shape at the right time. It was the era of the "second everything," when postwar prosperity made second televisions, second bathrooms, and second cars expected accoutrements of middle-class American life. Next, signs at the hardware store and ads in popular magazines declared, "Every family needs two homes!...one for the workweek, one for pure pleasure."[1] In the 1950s and 1960s, more Americans than ever before found a vacation home (once limited to the wealthy) within their reach. The increase in disposable income and free time, an economy driven by individual consumption, and a new cultural emphasis on recreation redefined leisure as a middle-class prerogative and contributed to the democratization of the vacation home.

Many of these homes were based upon forms traditional to wilderness settings—the log cabin and the clapboard cottage. On the opposite side were high-style boxes with flat roofs and glass facades, standing brazen against the landscape. But for those wanting a place that was innovative and exciting, modern yet warm, a place wholly suited to the informality of the new recreation lifestyle, a third alternative emerged.

Starting in the 1950s, the A-frame gained prominence as a popular vacation home type. Its appeal transcended geography and class in part because its form defied categorization. Was it the embodiment of contemporary geometric invention or a steadfast, timeless form, suggesting rustic survival? From grand versions overlooking Big Sur to the small plywood shacks advertised in *Field and Stream*, there was an A-frame for almost every budget. It was sturdy, easy to build, and seemed appropriate to any setting. Perhaps its greatest appeal was that it was different, an expression of individuality that meant relaxation and escape from the everyday, workaday world.

Triangular buildings did not always hold such connotations. "Roof huts" turned up in ancient China, on South Pacific islands, and throughout Europe, where they functioned as cooking houses, farm storage sheds, animal shelters, peasant cottages, and ceremonial structures. In the United States, the A-frame was a utilitarian form until after World War II.

After the war, a succession of architects found the A-frame to be an appropriately whimsical and informal stage on which to play out the still nebulous leisure lifestyle. Through their designs, the postwar A-frame, in all its myriad variations, took shape. The excitement aroused by these early designs attracted the attention of a building industry that had grown fat on the postwar housing boom and was looking for markets beyond the suburbs. National timber corporations and local lumberyards and contractors recognized the profits to be had in vacation homes. Partnering with mass-market magazines and home-design services, they promoted second homes in hundreds of articles, plan books, and do-it-yourself guidebooks. Because A-frames were instantly recognizable and appealed to a variety of demographic groups, they were often at the forefront of these initiatives. The appearance of prepackaged A-frame kits made an already simple structure even easier and cheaper to build, furthering its appeal and hastening its spread from coast to coast.

Soon, the A-frame was a national phenomenon. It dotted ski slopes from Stowe, Vermont, to Squaw Valley, California, and was a common sight in resort communities and forests and on back roads in between. Triangular pool cabanas, garden sheds, and playhouses brought a touch of the leisure lifestyle to the suburban backyard. By the early 1960s, the A-frame became a cultural icon, a geometric representation of the good life. Hoping to capitalize on this connotation, a variety of companies made A-frames the centerpiece of their advertising and promotional campaigns. Restaurants, gas stations, liquor stores, and a range of other businesses set up shop in triangular buildings, relying on the prominent shape to lure customers. A-frames were also adapted for hundreds of the new religious structures that accompanied the postwar move to the suburbs. Triangular restaurants and churches illustrated how the A-frame made its way beyond the lakeshore and the ski slope to influence wider architectural circles. At the same time they were indicative of the A-frame's increasing prominence in American culture.

The term *A-frame* has come to include any vacation home with a low-slung, steeply pitched roof. This broad interpretation suggests the depth to which the form has infused popular culture, but a narrower definition more closely reflects the term's meaning during the postwar period. An A-frame is a triangular structure with a series of rafters or trusses that are joined at the peak and descend outward to a main floor level, with no intervening vertical walls. The rafters are covered with a roof surface that ties the frames together and usually continues to the floor. Though some are steeper and a few are lower to the ground, most A-frames have roof rafters and floor joists of the same length, connected at sixty-degree angles to form an equilateral triangle.[2]

Rafters are connected to either woodsill plates at the floor level or, to take full advantage of the triangle's innate strength, are bolted to floor joists to form trusses. Most have horizontal collar beams that strengthen the frame and function as floor joists for a second-level loft. These cross ties, combined with the angled roof rafters, give the A-frame its name. Because gable walls are not load bearing, there are few limits to how they can be configured: open or enclosed, flat or prow-shaped, with or without doors.

In defining an A-frame, structural systems were less important than what a building looked like on the outside. Plenty of postwar A-frames were constructed without collar beams running across the center. Many houses skipped the framing altogether, using prefabricated modular panels instead. Historical forms were even more varied; some had central posts supporting ridge beams upon which the roof rafters were set. Others featured a boxlike interior framework over which rafters were leaned. Few, if any, ancient versions were constructed as trusses with rafters connected to floor joists.

Within the triangular form, however, there was considerable room for interpretation, adaptation, and variation. The A-frame's flexibility was one of its chief appeals. The simple shape could be easily altered to compensate for its innate drawbacks and to accommodate the preferences of individual owners. Dormers, vertical walls set within the diagonal rafters, and three or four gable designs were elements of a vocabulary that allowed for considerable individualization while retaining the basic triangular shape.[3]

The A-frame vacation home was accompanied by a collection of apparent dichotomies. Was it traditional or modern, highbrow or lowbrow, trendy or tacky? Custom-designed A-frames by architects trained at the Massachusetts Institute of Technology or by former apprentices

of Frank Lloyd Wright seem incongruous alongside the uncelebrated triangular shacks that
resulted from do-it-yourself projects. Perhaps for
this reason the A-frame has been largely over-
looked by historians. What seem like contradic-
tions, however, are really only characteristics of
the A-frame's once broad acceptance and widespread appeal.

Finding the fading embers of this boom—
in the archives and along the roadside—offers a
chance to explore the rise of postwar leisure culture, to see how modernism and other design
trends were accepted or rejected by the general
public, and to observe the ways marketing and
consumption patterns shape the built world. As
mid-century A-frames become increasingly rare,
it is important to understand how this form
became a nearly ubiquitous feature of the postwar leisure landscape, how it crossed into other
areas of architectural design, and why people
like David Perlman chose to spend their free
time in and around them. In the end, this exploration can help us figure out why such an
unusual little building caused such a big stir
and what the A-frame boom tells us about the
postwar era.

David Perlman's A-frame, 2003

Chapter 1

A-frame Antecedents (to 1950)

THE A-FRAME IS NOT A NEW IDEA:
THE FIRST MAN WHO LEANED TWO
POLES TOGETHER AND THREW A SKIN
OVER THEM HAD A RUDIMENTARY
VERSION OF IT. —*TIME*, DECEMBER 1961

Magazine articles and plan books from the 1950s and 1960s often introduced the A-frame with claims of an ancient lineage. It was likened to the tepee, to trapper's cabins, Canadian ski shelters, and Swiss chalets. But postwar A-frame designers did not base their work on historical research, and they were not particularly interested in accurately replicating earlier triangular forms. Because of its simple, intuitive shape, designers, writers, and owners just assumed there had to be an A-frame tradition.[1]

Attempts at fixing a pedigree had two motives. First, by suggesting that A-frames had existed in varying forms for centuries, the radical nature of the design was made more acceptable and marketable. The connection also illustrated how the postwar triangular vacation home differed from its predecessors. An article about the first mass-produced A-frame kit stated, "Although the tent like shape of the Leisure House goes back to prehistoric times, the methods and materials used in building it are strictly latter 20th century."[2] Another claimed that "in silhouette, the wood A-frame is strikingly reminiscent of the ancient Indian tepee. In all other respects, it's ultra-modern and well suited for vacation abodes."[3]

Historical examples of the triangular building shed light on claims made by postwar A-frame boosters. They show that the A-frame's adaptability, so much a selling point for postwar versions, was not new to this period. Early triangular structures illustrate how humans, separated in some cases by thousands of years and vast cultural and environmental differences, were drawn to the same basic form. A-frame construction was attractive in ancient Japan and medieval England for the same reasons it was to designers of vacation homes in the postwar era. They were all striving for an easy way to con-

Victor von Gegerfelt's hunting lodge for the Gothenburg Fair, Gothenburg, Sweden, 1871, detail

struct a secure dwelling, one that would derive remarkable strength from the least amount of material. Also, like their postwar descendants, early A-frame builders attached important cultural symbolism to their designs, meanings far beyond utility and convenience.

If the A-frame was an early human response to the need for shelter, where did it fit into the evolution of construction? There appears to be little agreement among historians, anthropologists, and archaeologists.[4] Architectural historians, including Vitruvius, Marc-Antoine Laugier, and Gottfried Semper, preferred to think that humans progressed straight from the cave to a building with four columns and a pitched roof. Such primitive huts—made of timber, bundled reeds, or stone—were considered predecessors of the classical Greek temple. More recent studies in construction history likewise overlook a role for the triangular shelter.[5]

Because they were made of wood and often built low to the ground, ancient triangular structures have not survived. Excavated postholes, mounds and dens, clay models found in tombs, images on pottery shards, and residual building traditions provide the clues. Whether the triangular shelter was an intermediary between the cave and post-and-lintel construction will likely remain unknown. A possible progression, however, is suggested by the Neolithic architecture of Japan and China. There historians have found evidence that the pitched roof began as a separate structure, independent of vertical walled buildings later added below it.

In northern China triangular shelters may have first functioned as coverings for pit dwellings. They were part cave, part structure, one step away from sprouting vertical walls. Theories on building developments in other parts of Neolithic China suggest that the

pitched-roof and post-and-beam forms descended from the trees rather than growing upward. The prototype was an equilateral triangle with a thatched roof, covering a platform set in the branches of a tree. Successive versions were increasingly elaborate—tree trunks became posts that supported the building and framed vertical walls—until it came to resemble Chinese forms still seen today.[6]

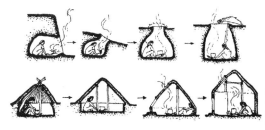

Hypothetical development of early Chinese dwellings from cave to post-and-beam structure, with triangle shelter as intermediary step

Several sources on Japanese building traditions claim that prehistoric inhabitants of that island built structures known as *tenchi-kongen tsukuri,* or literally, "a palace construction of heaven and earth."[7] The basic structure consisted of two vertical pillars at either end, supporting and connected by a ridgepole. Rafters extended from the ground to the ridgepole (and beyond), forming the basic triangular shape. A number of horizontal purlinlike members, attached to the rafters along the length of the structure, supported a final layer of straw or reed thatch. Historians suspect that, like the Chinese version, this structure was originally set over a semisubterranean pit.[8] Also like its Chinese counterpart, the *tenchi-kongen* evolved upward over many centuries, as it was raised off the ground and placed atop vertical walls. This arrangement eventually found its way into spiritual architecture, most

LEFT Stages of development of *tenchi-kongen*

LEFT **Council of Vailoatai, in costume, outside the house of Chief Tuatagaloa, American Samoa**
RIGHT **Pole-and-thatch house on a raised platform, Wakdi Island, New Guinea**

notably in the Shinto shrines at Ise. Though torn down and rebuilt every generation, the shrines still exhibit the predominant thatched roof and intersecting rafters.

As the Ise shrines suggest, roofs have long carried special significance in Japan.[9] In residences, their height and decoration were important symbols of an owner's position and wealth. This was especially true in the remote and mountainous Shirakawa district, where traditional farmhouses were built with enormous sixty-degree pitched roofs, which contained three of the four floors. Historian Bruno Taut, who saw simple Japanese houses as the pure progenitors of twentieth-century modernism, believed that the Shirakawa houses developed from "primitive huts, which merely consist of a similar roof with an inclination of about sixty degrees without any vertical ground wall." Taut included in his discussion photographs of two structures, a "shed under a straw roof without walls" and "a hut without walls," fishing shacks and field shelters that bear a close resemblance to the *tenchi-kongen*. [10]

All-roof triangular structures also figure in the building traditions of New Guinea and islands in western Polynesia. Used as residential structures, communal houses, and ceremonial "great houses," the thatched pole buildings featured prominent grass-covered roofs, which often had sagging "saddleback" ridges and outward-sloping gables. Some anthropologists see them as cultural symbols of the boat, an important Pacific conveyance. Houses with the tallest, steepest roofs, on Indonesia's Flores Island for example, were said to appear like wind-filled sails.[11] Again, these forms evolved over time, sprouting posts, platforms, and eventually vertical walls, to resemble more recent housing found throughout the region.

TONGS AND CRUCKS

On the other side of the world, at approximately the same time, Europeans were building structures that are also clear antecedents of the twentieth-century A-frame vacation home. One form, labeled by historians a "primary tong-support framework," consisted of two pairs of inclined timbers, crossing at the top where they supported a ridgepole.[12] Most basic designs used only two supports, one at either end; larger structures, like the twentieth-century A-frame, had multiple tong frames, arranged at intervals along the length of the structure.[13] In both cases, the angled timbers rested on stone pads or were set directly into the ground without a floor or cross ties to strengthen them. Grass thatch was used to cover the roof and gable ends. Archaeological investigations across Europe have uncovered the remnants of angled postholes, indicating the presence of triangular structures as far back as the Stone Age. Over the next several millennia, this type of construction spread throughout the continent. In Germany the structures were known as *dach-hutten*, or "roof huts"; in Scandinavia they were called *skåle*.[14]

Triangular buildings were of great interest to Swedish folklorist Sigurd Erixon. During the 1940s he documented the variety of surviving triangular structures throughout Sweden, a collection he grouped under the term *sadeltakshus*, or "saddle-roof houses." Structurally, these buildings were similar to one another: rafters, covered with thatch or wood planks, linked at the roof peak and resting on single-course stone foundations. Gables were enclosed with vertical planks. The *sadeltakshus* were agricultural buildings. Usually part of a larger farm complex, they functioned as storehouses, sheep sheds, woodsheds, or horse stables. Although the

buildings that Erixon found while doing his field research dated only to the mid-nineteenth century, he saw in them connections to forms that were much older.[15]

It is likely that Saxon invaders brought triangular framing to the British Isles.[16] A fourteenth-century illuminated manuscript, "The Romance of Alexander," shows a triangular structure set alongside a market stall. The roof of the building was made of thatch or branches, and a plank door with strap hinges opened from the otherwise solid gable end. Though shown next to a tent with bread for sale, it is not clear whether the triangular building functioned as a market shelter that was temporary or portable or whether it was a permanent dwelling.[17]

Around this time a new all-roof building form with roots in triangular construction evolved in the British midlands and northwest. Cruck buildings were distinguished by the use of naturally curved timbers, or blades, for the main rafters.[18] To form the curving framework, a tree trunk was stripped of all of its branches except the lowest and thickest. The trunk and branch were then hewn and split in half. Each half was placed upright, facing the other, and secured at the peak by a ridgepole. In larger versions a collar beam was used to further strengthen the frame. As in the tong-support, large structures used a row of crucks while small cottages and sheds required only a pair on either end.[19]

Basic cruck construction gave rise to several variations, including examples in which the frame sprung not from ground level but from midway up a vertical wall. Lack of headroom (the bane of the twentieth-century A-frame homeowners' existence) was probably a primary factor in the progression to more elaborate cruck framing. Later versions became the basis for roof systems used to cover great halls, churches,

TOP LEFT Nineteenth-century Swedish *vedskjul* (woodshed), documented by Sigurd Erixon; TOP CENTER Swedish horse stable in the "saddle-roof house" form dating to the mid-nineteenth century, documented by Sigurd Erixon in the 1940s; TOP RIGHT The exposed end wall of Avon Cottage in Hampshire, England, reveals the curving blades of a cruck frame; RIGHT Tong-support structure in "The Romance of Alexander," circa 1340

Teapot Hall, Lincolnshire, England, 1930

barns, and houses, many of which left the crucks visible on half-timbered gable ends.[20] Eventually, as the large trees required for blades became more difficult to obtain and when second stories became common, crucks were supplanted by post-and-truss construction.

But the practice of triangular building did not disappear entirely from the English landscape. In 1870, at Scrivelsby in Lincolnshire, a village wheelwright and joiner named Edwin Jobson built an all-roof structure with straight pine rafters, a combination thatch-and-slate roof, and plaster over wattle-and-daub gable ends. Called Teapot Hall, because its dormer resembled a handle and the chimney a spout, the design featured a small living room and kitchen on the ground floor, a bedroom on an upper level (reached through a trap door), and a second ground-floor bedroom in a later addition.[21]

Tourists and even historians who visited Teapot Hall assumed it dated to the Middle Ages. Kathleen Wood, who lived there as a child, recalled, "We had sightseers from far and wide even in those days who used to say, 'Isn't it love-

ly.' Mother's answer was always: 'You wouldn't think so if you had to live in it.' It was very difficult to arrange furniture because of the way the walls sloped inward. We had lived in some very primitive places but Teapot Hall was the worst of all." Others remembered a rhyme associated with the building: "Teapot Hall, Teapot Hall, All roof and no wall."[22]

In 1935 the last tenant moved out, and Teapot Hall became a refuge for squatters. A decade later it met its end, despite attempts by the Society for the Protection of Ancient Buildings to preserve it. On August 23, 1945, the night Japan surrendered and World War II came to a close, a group of American airmen were celebrating at a local pub. On their way home, along Teapot Lane they stumbled upon the abandoned cottage. A collapsing shell of dried grass and woven sticks, Teapot Hall proved too much of a temptation for the airmen, who set it on fire with a flare and burnt it to the ground.

While the Wood family thought it unfortunate to live in a triangular house, there were others who considered an A-frame ideal. In 1927 English writer A. A. Milne shared tales of Christopher Robin, Winnie-the-Pooh, and their friends from the Hundred Acre Wood, in his book *The House at Pooh Corner.* The first story, "A House Is Built at Pooh Corner for Eeyore," recounts efforts one wintry day to keep the dour donkey Eeyore sheltered from the snow. After Eeyore's house goes missing (because Piglet and Pooh mistakenly dismantle it to use the sticks to build a house for Eeyore), he is overjoyed to discover what he thinks is his misplaced house nearby:

> It just goes to show what can be done
> by taking a little trouble," said Eeyore.
> "Do you see, Pooh? Do you see, Piglet?
> Brains first and then Hard Work. Look
> at it! That's the way to build a house,"
> said Eeyore proudly."[23]

Eeyore's fictitious house along with the real versions of triangular construction were built for the exigency of shelter and survival. They were the vernacular of the part-time builder. Teapot Hall was an early appropriation of the all-roof tradition for the sake of nostalgia. A more focused attempt was undertaken around the same time by a Swedish architect named Victor von Gegerfelt. Practicing in and around Gothenburg during the second half of the nineteenth century, Gegerfelt was concerned with developing a Nordic style of wood construction, one evocative of age-old forms though based on innovative construction techniques and technologies. His designs for hospitals, schools, villas, and other residences put him at the forefront of a Norse revival. [24]

In the 1870s he began to experiment with an approach to building he called the "stave-triangle system." These ideas were worked through in a number of designs, including exhibition buildings for an 1871 agricultural fair in Gothenburg, a fish market, and several villas. Between 1908 and 1914, Gegerfelt articulated the principles and provenance of his stave-triangle system in a treatise titled "A Saga of Some Old and Recent Buildings."[25] In the handwritten manuscript, Gegerfelt traced his inspiration to German theories of iron bridge framing and old Norse stave churches, belfries, and assembly halls. He may also have been influenced by military buildings, like the Värmland Regiment barracks that he encountered during an earlier career in the army. Gegerfelt essentially rediscovered the saddle-roof house, finding in its basic shape structural efficacy, visual pleasure, and the resonance of a pure Scandinavian building tradition.

As late as the 1950s, the descendants of saddle-roof houses, tong frames, crucks, and other triangular buildings were still in use throughout Germany and Scandinavia, the Low Countries, Britain, Spain, and Italy as barns,

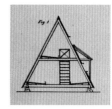

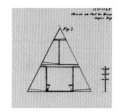

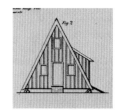

LEFT **From *The Complete Tales of Winnie-the-Pooh* by A. A. Milne, illustrated by E.H. Shepard;** RIGHT **Drawings for the Värmland Regiment Barracks, showing two rows of bunks on the lower level and a single row in the loft, Värmland, Sweden, 1837**

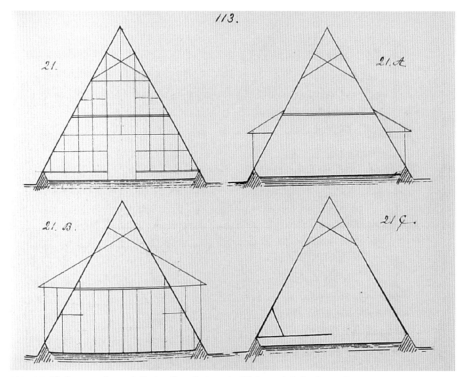

TOP LEFT **Victor von Gegerfelt, hunting lodge, built for a fair in Copenhagen, Denmark,1872;** TOP RIGHT **Gegerfelt's hunting lodge for the Gothenburg Fair, Gothenburg, Sweden, 1871;** BOTTOM **Pages from Gegerfelt's manuscript "A Saga of Some Old and Recent Buildings," presenting various configurations for an A-frame barn**

sheep shelters, summer cooking sheds, cellar roofs, and other outbuildings. [26] During his pre–World War I study of Belgian folk buildings, historian C. F. Innocent came across a small, recently constructed "farm store" based upon the tong support.[27] While traveling through Hungary shortly after World War II, photographer Werner Bischoff photographed a triangular farm hut with a thatched roof and wattle-and-daub gable ends. The image appeared in *Life* magazine in 1947.[28] Like Sigurd Erixon's Swedish sadeltakshus, these buildings were at least a hundred years old, vestiges of earlier traditions that had survived to the twentieth century. They may have served as inspiration for a burst of triangular building construction in the first decades of the twentieth century. Architects Carl Weidemeyer and Ernst May in Germany and Paul Artaria in Switzerland developed triangular cottages meant to look vernacular and old. Imbuing the form with a nostalgic nationalism, they proposed it as a response to the post–World War I housing shortage and as the first holiday retreats.[29]

Examples of Swiss triangular structures are of particular interest because postwar A-frame vacation homes were often referred to as Swiss cottages or Swiss chalets and their origins were assumed to be Alpine. A-frames with carved balcony spindles and embellished eaves (features borrowed from chalets found in Switzerland's Bern Canton) strengthened that connection in many minds. But outside the experimentation of Paul Artaria and others in the early twentieth century, all-roof structures were not a prominent part of the Alpine building heritage. While the Swiss chalet and A-frame were both defined by the shape and dominance of their roof forms, the typical chalet had a wide, gentle slope, in marked contrast to the A-frame's steeper pitch.[30]

The triangular form was the basis for innumerable structures built throughout human history. Its appeal lay in the speed and ease with which it could be constructed, its strength, and its durability. The A-frame's symbolism was plastic, readily molded by different groups into sundry meanings. Appreciating its utility, humans continued to turn to the triangular form for shelters and sheds well into the twentieth century.[31] Because the design is so intuitive and because its construction was so ephemeral, tracing its development over many centuries and continents can only be episodic. That triangular structures were built as protection against Swedish winters and Indonesian monsoons, as an authentic vernacular tradition, and as a later evocation of such traditions shows the versatility of the form and its enduring appeal.

23

Hut near Debrecen, Hungary, 1947

24

A-FRAMES IN AMERICA

In the United States, the A-frame had long been used for ice houses, pump houses, field shelters, and chicken coops. In 1904 writer and outdoorsman Dan Beard wrote an article for *Outing* magazine in which he proposed several rustic wilderness huts for "the city man who camps in winter for a short holiday in the woods." The Mossback and the Pontiac were temporary triangular shelters, built with logs, sticks, and green birch bark, that Beard claimed were based upon log tents used by Native Americans in the Northwest.[32] Prefiguring the postwar connection with winter sports, triangular sheds were also used to cover the rope-tow machinery on an early ski slope.[33] They were fine for temporary shelters for animals and for storing things, but they were not often lived in by choice. This changed in 1934, when Rudolph Schindler designed a triangular cabin for Gisela Bennati in the hills above Lake Arrowhead, California. Though not well remembered, his design set forth all of the essential elements that later came to characterize the postwar A-frame vacation home.

Schindler left his native Austria and arrived in the United States in 1914. Like many Central European architects and artists at the time, Schindler was attracted by new opportunities in America, hopeful for a climate more receptive to modernism and eager to escape a continent on the verge of war. Three years after Schindler arrived in Chicago, Frank Lloyd Wright hired him; he participated in several of Wright's commissions, including the Imperial Hotel in Tokyo and Aline Barnsdall's Hollyhock House in Los Angeles. By 1922 Schindler had relocated for a final time, lured to booming Los Angeles. His move came just as Southern California was gaining a reputation as a filmmaking and artistic center and as a haven for innovative architectural design. Two of

Schindler's most significant works were completed during his first years in California, his studio-residence and a beach house for health guru Philip Lovell. Working with glass walls, right angles, flat roofs, and open plans, Schindler adapted these expressions of modern design to the climate and lifestyle of Southern California. Some of his other early work, however, shows a greater willingness to transgress the International Style's orthodoxy in trying out unusual roof pitches and planes.

Schindler's first design to incorporate a

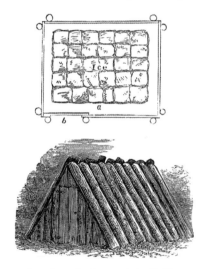

American icehouse, late 1800s

steeply pitched roof was a modest house developed for Laura Davies in Los Angeles between 1922 and 1924. During the same period he drew plans for another, more elaborate triangle-based design, for M. Davis Baker of Hollywood. Both projects combined living areas beneath a triangular roof structure with flat-roofed spaces—dormers on the Davies house and a series of cubic and linear projections spilling out around

Native American log tents, about 1820–50

The Mossback, 1904

The Pontiac, 1904

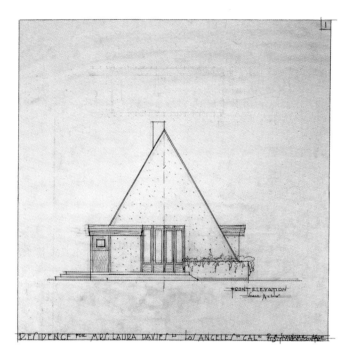

RESIDENCE FOR MRS. LAURA DAVIES - LOS ANGELES - CAL - R. M. SCHINDLER, ARCH

R.M. Schindler, Residence for Laura Davies, entrance elevation, 1922–24

the Baker house. The Davies design, in particular, foreshadowed postwar A-frames in its scale and simplicity of form. Curiously, the interior was not open to the full height of the roof, but enclosed beneath a flat ceiling.[34]

For unknown reasons, the Davies and Baker designs never made it off the drawing board. Schindler set aside the idea of a dominant triangular roof only to return to it ten years later in the vacation home design for Gisela Bennati. The house was erected on a wooded mountain slope above Lake Arrowhead, a resort community seventy-five miles east of Los Angeles. It was one of the first known all-roof vacation homes in the United States and in many ways indistinguishable from the thousands of A-frames that followed.

Schindler summed up the design by saying, "The formal vocabulary is based on the triangle and kept in a playful mood throughout."[35] A series of sixty-degree triangular trusses, tied laterally by collar beams and resting on a masonry base, formed the structural frame. The main living- and dining-room areas occupied the forward portion of the interior, with two separate levels behind. On the ground level rear, Schindler placed a garage within the A-frame shape; above was a bunkroom and a pair of bedrooms, one with a balcony overlooking the living room. As in later vacation home designs, the sloping rafters extending the full height of the living room were left exposed, to emphasize the high ceiling and to increase the feeling of spaciousness. Schindler's efforts to reflect the

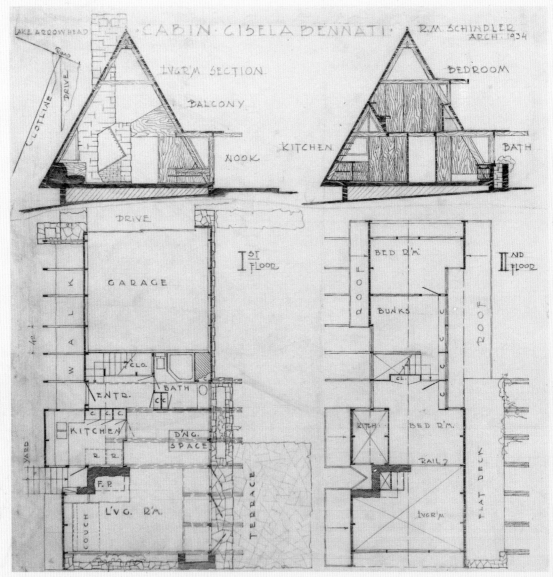

R.M. Schindler, Bennati House project drawing, 1934

home's steeply pitched roof on the interior was typical of his general approach to design. Architectural historian David Leclerc has observed the result: "By the late 1930s, the roof is so engaged in the shaping of the interior space that the traditional distinction between wall and roof disappears: the house becomes its roof."[36]

Schindler did not invent the triangular form, but he did bring it into the modern era. The types of building materials, the way they were used, and the interior plan seen in the Bennati house set precedents that so many postwar vacation home designers repeated (in most cases with no knowledge of Schindler's contribution). Schindler's design relied heavily on exposed plywood, most notably in the ceiling and the interior partitions. He placed the main living room, complete with a stone fireplace, beneath the large open area immediately adjacent to the large gable window. The kitchen, bath, and service areas were located in secondary spaces beneath the loft. This spatial arrangement was typical of the majority of postwar A-frames. Of Schindler's A-frame innovations, the glazed gable end was the most enduring. By finishing the main end wall entirely in glass, Schindler blurred the distinction between inside and outside, flooding the interior with sunlight and dramatic views out. Combined with other vertical windows, set in dormers and inset walls, the design produced an airiness and buoyancy that balanced the heavy appearance of the roof. The Bennati house was essentially a postwar A-frame vacation home, built twenty years ahead of its time.

Historian Dominique Rouillard has argued that the interest in unusual roof lines drove Schindler's design more than any external factor.[37] It was a fascination with geometric forms, a desire to reflect the sloping, pine tree–studded

Bennati House exterior

site, and a willingness to venture beyond the boundaries of the International Style that led Schindler to the A-frame.[38] Beyond providing visual and spatial interest, Schindler had an additional motive for his A-frame design. Lake Arrowhead was a private development. Its lots were subject to the requirement that all new construction be designed in the "Norman style." At the time such stipulations were a common defense against the encroachment of flat-roofed

Bennati House interior

modern homes. Working within these vague confines, Schindler revisited his earlier experiments with the all-roof concept, presented the result as an example of typical Norman construction, and got it past the review committee.[39]

Schindler's A-frame received some belated coverage in the architectural press. Perhaps most notable was a four-page article about the house in the California modernist magazine, *Arts and Architecture* published in 1944.[40] Two years later the British *Architect's Journal* presented the design around the same time that photos of it appeared in a London exhibition on regional buildings in the United States.[41] Despite some publicity and similarities between it and the A-frames that came after, the Bennati house was rarely, if ever, mentioned as a source of inspiration for later designs. Instead the ancestry was repeatedly traced to ancient forms and modest sheds and shacks.

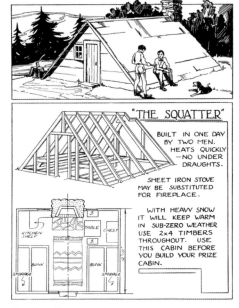

"THE SQUATTER"

BUILT IN ONE DAY BY TWO MEN. HEATS QUICKLY — NO UNDER DRAUGHTS.

SHEET IRON STOVE MAY BE SUBSTITUTED FOR FIREPLACE.

WITH HEAVY SNOW IT WILL KEEP WARM IN SUB-ZERO WEATHER USE 2×4 TIMBERS THROUGHOUT. USE THIS CABIN BEFORE YOU BUILD YOUR PRIZE CABIN.

The Squatter, a basic shelter designed by Conrad Meinecke, 1945

Even at the dawn of the vacation home boom in the late 1940s, basic triangular wilderness shelters still had much more to do with backcountry survival than the leisure attitudes anticipated by the Bennati house. A 1945 book titled *Your Cabin in the Woods* proposed one rustic design called the Squatter, which, the author stated, would make an appropriate starter cabin before the "prize cabin" was completed. In this design, and in the many similar structures that were no doubt built but not publicized, the triangular shape was appreciated more for its utility than its aesthetics.[42]

A-frame enthusiasts in the 1950s and 1960s were correct in asserting that the form had an ancient lineage. The simplicity, strength, and versatility of tong-support, cruck, and other triangular structures explain why they were so common for so many centuries. Designers of twentieth-century A-frame vacation homes were drawn to the form for the same reasons. The fourteenth-century peasant shown in "The Romance of Alexander" manuscript would surely recognize the postwar A-frame vacation home, even if its new function was incomprehensible.

Early A-frames varied in the function and cultural significance ascribed to them. Samoan villagers saw the towering "great house" as a projection of authority and a symbol of the boat's central role in their lives. To German, Swedish, and Swiss designers in the late 1800s and early 1900s, the A-frame represented a vernacular folk tradition that inspired feelings of national pride. In the 1950s, the triangular building was adopted and adapted yet again. The function was more frivolous than in the past (once a tool for basic survival, it was now a setting for barbecues and cocktails), yet many Americans found meaning in the A-frame. In the postwar era triangular vacation homes came to represent new leisure attitudes, an otherworldly lifestyle of active enjoyment and gratification.

The Right Shape at the Right Time

THAT "LITTLE PLACE IN THE COUNTRY" HAS
TURNED INTO A BILLION-DOLLAR-A-YEAR BUSINESS,
POWERFUL ENOUGH TO INSPIRE RADICAL CHANGES
IN BUILDING METHODS AND THE MOST EXCITING
DOMESTIC ARCHITECTURE BEING CREATED IN
AMERICA TODAY. —*SPORTS ILLUSTRATED*, 1963

The A-frame's ascent to popularity coincided with an economic expansion that brought vacation homes within reach of a rapidly expanding middle class. As Americans began to enjoy longer weekends and extended vacations, they yearned to get away from their everyday life, to obtain what was once available only to the rich: a second home in the country. There was a new emphasis on recreation, both for self-improvement and for the sheer joy of it. With the evolution of a leisure industry predicated on conspicuous consumption, Americans packed up the station wagon and headed out to stake their claim on a small lakeshore or hillside lot.

Architecture during this time was also undergoing change. Blending elements of modernism, local building traditions, and recent technological advances, architects, especially those on the West Coast, developed entirely new expressions: origami-like roof forms, space-age motifs, and creative glazing schemes. Bearing the influence of work by Frank Lloyd Wright, Eliel Saarinen, William Wurster, and others, these designs offered a more human contemporary architecture and appealed to broad segments of the American population. Some of the most creative designs were for vacation homes.

Free from the strictures of the permanent home, second-home design offered architects a cheap, informal opportunity to try something new and garner attention. Image-conscious clients saw the contemporary vacation home as a way to attract notice, to distance themselves from everyday life, and to reflect their true unbuttoned personality. Owning a stunning vacation home marked the achievement of

Vacation homes and boats were the tools of leisure ar.d the signs of success

a revised American dream. It was into this mix of economic, architectural, and cultural trends that the A-frame came to the fore.

The A-frame's popularity lasted from around 1950 through the first half of the 1970s. This twenty-five-year period saw an upswell in the financial fortunes of many Americans. During the 1950s, as industry shifted from wartime production to the manufacture of consumer goods and as the economy ballooned, an increasing number of families had more discretionary income and leisure time.[1] Economic prosperity fostered a rapid expansion of the postwar middle class. Between 1955 and 1965, the average income of an American worker rose fifty percent, while total disposable income increased fifty-seven percent.[2] Returned veterans, helped along by the GI Bill, created and filled a variety of new (largely white-collar) jobs in corporations, government bureaucracies, service industries, the media, and the military-industrial complex. As the percentage of middle-class families rose, their role and influence as culture creators grew proportionally.[3]

When the middle class began to dominate leisure spending, a new breed of vacation homes evolved to fit their budgets and accommodate their lifestyle. A nascent leisure industry, encompassing the building trades, real estate agents, magazine editors, and sporting good and motor vehicle manufacturers, promoted vacation homes as a necessary possession. The second home became a rightful inheritance.

Extravagant claims about the investment potential of vacation homes were part of the pitch. Payments were manageable, and appreciation was assumed. In the short term, renting out the home when not in use could cover much of the monthly mortgage payment. Long term, vacation homes could eventually serve as retirement homes before being passed on to one's children. According to some boosters, middle-class families could hardly afford not to own a second home. "As a rule...annual family vacations at resort hotels are a heavy drain on the budget, entail tiresome preparation and too often result in little more than fast-fading tans and fleeting memories. When such credits and debits are balanced, a vacation home may well be an economy."[4]

Rising incomes provided much of the capital needed to afford a vacation home, but many families still came up short. Increasingly available credit and financing helped close the gap.[5] Large, fully insulated homes in established resort communities or prime vacation locations were usually no problem, but banks were less willing to extend mortgages to individually constructed modest vacation homes on scattered lots, especially those built only for seasonal use.[6] Early on, bankers considered A-frames and other contemporary vacation houses a trend that would eventually lose favor and be difficult to resell in the event of foreclosure. The initial reluctance of banks to underwrite mortgages led producers and developers to offer financing directly and include credit applications as part of brochures and plan books. Advertisements for the precut A-frame kits encouraged buyers to "build now and pay later."[7]

Just when many Americans found themselves with more money to spend on nonessentials, they also secured more free time in which to spend it. By the postwar period, the forty-hour work week was nearly universal, the culmination of a trend dating back to the beginning of the century. In 1940 the average American worker was entitled to one week of paid vacation and two paid holidays per year. By 1969, the length of the average paid vacation had doubled

Excavation for Interstate 80
between San Francisco and
Lake Tahoe

Construction of Interstate 80
in Illinois

and the number of paid holidays had grown fivefold.[8] Saturdays were fully ensconced as part of a full weekend, rather than the last (half) day of the work week.

Other factors contributed to a boom in vacation home ownership. The creation of artificial lakes and reservoirs by private developers and public agencies like the Bureau of Reclamation opened tens of thousands of miles of new shoreline to recreational use.[9] Between 1946 and 1966, the mileage of surface road in the United States doubled.[10] Highway construction, especially the new interstate system, brought large undeveloped recreation areas within a Friday night's drive of the city and suburb. Roads like Interstate 70, through the Colorado Rockies and Interstate 80, through the Sierra Nevada Mountains between San Francisco and Reno, created weekend wonderlands that were accessible year-round.[11]

Since it first became affordable to middle-class Americans, allowing them to reach beyond railroad-serviced resort areas, the automobile had spurred the dispersal of recreational activities. In the 1920s and 1930s, cabin camps and cottage courts sprouted up along the roadside, offering a more individual, private, and flexible leisure experience.[12] Vacation homes, especially those individually built on scattered lots, took that seclusion a step further, requiring interaction only with other family members and invited guests.[13] New roads and the increasingly ubiquitous car permitted vacation home owners and builders

to seek out a private piece of unspoiled and uncrowded paradise.

From their earliest introduction as a postwar vacation house form, A-frames were well suited to the new economic and cultural atmosphere. A-frame designers in particular were determined to keep costs down in order to attract people of more modest financial means. Though grand versions were built, the A-frame was more often seen as a natural "entry level" vacation home. Plan books and popular magazines like *Better Homes and Gardens* and *House Beautiful* featured a variety of small, six-hundred- to thousand-square-foot A-frames, their dramatic shape compensating for their diminutive size. Construction costs were often kept around ten dollars per square foot; construction time was measured in weekends. Articles boasted of how easy, fast, and inexpensive the A-frame was to build, one stating that "with a few long poles and not much dough, you can build your own Shangri-la."[14] The A-frame contributed to the promise that through economic prosperity and the beneficence of American capitalism, everyone could have access to the good life.

LEISURE TIME AND VACATION HOMES

Postwar leisure culture was an amalgam of several, at times conflicting, attitudes. There was an established and stubbornly persistent belief that free time was best spent on self-improvement, whether it was taking adult education courses or attending the ballet. Alternately, there was a sense that postwar Americans had earned the right to relaxation, to lounge in hammocks and share cocktails on the patio. Somewhere between these two poles was an increasingly predominant interest in spending free time actively engaged in physical, usually outdoor, recreation.

The many faces of postwar recreation, from *Care-Free Living*, a plan book published by the Homasote Company

The Ranger from the Douglas Fir Plywood Association plan book, 1962

Middle-class expansion, its accompanying buying power, and the rise of a true mass culture were the primary engines that reordered the character of leisure. The wealthy no longer dominated free-time spending and no longer dictated public perceptions of what constituted the leisure life. Instead the rules were being rewritten by a new, broader group of tastemakers and popularized by the mass media. *Fortune* magazine summed up the trend saying that "the yacht splurge of the late 1920s is replaced by the outboard boom of today."[15] Unlike the yacht, the outboard motorboat represented widespread access to waterskiing, fishing, and a lakeside vacation home.

Broadly considered, leisure is a state of mind, a freedom from the necessities of life. It is the attitudes and activities we choose to fill the time not spent working, sleeping, or doing any-

thing else essential to survival. Since the nineteenth century, when industrialization first delineated work time from free time and that free time became more available to those of modest means, there was a growing concern among social scientists, politicians, and religious leaders that American civilization was imperiled by leisure.[16] This fear reached a peak in the postwar era. Robert Hutchins, a former president of the University of Chicago, observed at the time that "if we survive the leisure which the atomic age will bring, it may make peace more horrible than war. We face the dreadful prospect of hour after hour, even day after day, with nothing to do. After we read all the comic books, traveled all the miles, seen all the movies, what shall we do then?"[17]

Many worried not so much about a nation of bored sybarites but one made weak from lazy living, a population grown soft on luxury. In the Cold War era of missile gaps and domino theories, this was especially dangerous. The rhetoric of the time posed the Soviet Union, tempered by war and adversity, against an America that was becoming too comfortable to bother defending itself. If Americans chose to squander their increasing leisure time on amusements, entertainment, diversions, time wasters, or time fillers, the moral and physical vitality of the entire country would be jeopardized. Abundance, rather than a symbol of the victory of the American system, would be its downfall.

The only solution was the worthwhile use of leisure, spending free time on activities considered fulfilling and enriching, ones that restored and regenerated. Wholesome leisure, from learning to paint or play a musical instrument to hiking and woodworking and building one's own vacation home, refreshed one for new work and new trials psychologically, physically, and spiritually. In this way the benefits of worthwhile leisure activities extended far beyond the individual. Wholesome leisure emphasized the centrality of the family and created an educated, cultured population.[18] It was an antidote to such un-American developments as urbanization, overcrowding, automation, and rapid change. It was often hard work and, therefore, an extension of the Protestant ethic that exhorted labor and spurned indolence.

Although postwar leisure meant different things to different people, almost all saw it as an opportunity for consumption. Whether it was a pair of downhill skis, a dirt bike, rec room, or vacation home, spending money was a central component of the postwar leisure life. Like a Ford Mustang bought in addition to the family car, vacation homes were a signal to all that one had arrived, that success had been achieved, and that the leisure life was at hand. One recre-

ation area developer told a conference of builders that when it comes to vacation homes, status "is the sizzle you are selling."[19]

The best wholesome leisure activities were ones that encouraged consumption and furthered economic growth. Unlike passive entertainment—frequenting bars and other uses of free time derided by the experts—physical outdoor recreation activities and do-it-yourself projects required the purchase of increasingly specialized equipment and tools. Building vacation homes had beneficent effects that spread far beyond the real estate and construction industries, since second homes required a second set of sheets, silverware, and furniture.

Such views helped justify the enormous efforts federal, state, and local governments expended on increasing leisure opportunities. From establishing the Bureau of Outdoor Recreation to opening up Forest Service tracts to "vacation home-steading," government agencies worked to instill the ideal of productive leisure in American society.[20] Vacation homes, including A-

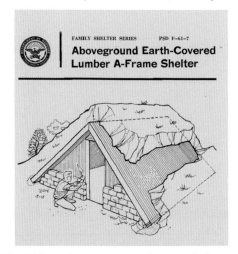

FAMILY SHELTER SERIES   PSD F–61–7

Aboveground Earth-Covered Lumber A-Frame Shelter

ABOVE **Aboveground A-frame bomb shelter, designed to protect as many as ten people from the effects of radioactive fallout, 1962;** RIGHT **The Engelmann Spruce, an A-frame plan by the Western Wood Products Association featured in** *Vacationland Homes,* **1960**

A-frames were the refuge where tired leisure seekers could retreat after a long day recreating, Alpine Villages brochure, c. 1963

of living that many felt they had earned after the privations of the Depression and self-denial of the war years, or at least after a hard week of work at the office. This was leisure as lifestyle, a concept that described the values of what one historian called "a new middle class of college-bred administrators, professionals and managers" who were oriented to a culture of "play, fun and excitement" and who took "endless delight in pursuing a lighthearted existence of interpersonal repartee and pleasure based on a moral code that bore no relationship to babbitry and its Protestant morality."[22] It was youth-oriented, individualistic, and unapologetic in its focus on gratification.

A-frames, and vacation homes in general, appealed to both button-down conformists and hedonistic pleasure seekers. A-frames straddled the line between the safety and conservatism of the family and the emergent swinging bachelor and independent single girl, between the moral obligation for wholesome recreation and the shameless quest for fun. A-frames were a sanctum where the nuclear family could retreat, find shelter, and immerse itself in the regenerative powers of nature. Alternately, the triangular vacation home could be a totem for nonconformity, the quintessential bachelor pad and singles' love nest, a place where unchaperoned romance could blossom on the bearskin rug before a prefabricated fireplace.[23]

DO-IT-YOURSELF

Families that built their own A-frames fulfilled the social scientist's and politician's hopes that Cold War Americans would make active and productive use of their free time. Amateur builders were part of a do-it-yourself phenomenon that included a plethora of activities from arts and crafts to building bookshelves and bar-

frames, were clearly seen as a bulwark against a creeping Communism and a soft citizenry. They were an assertion both of the primacy of the family and of private property. A-frames were literally adapted for the protection of the American family against a Cold War turned hot when in 1965 the Office of Civil Defense began testing triangular fallout shelters.[21]

In contrast to the view that leisure obligatorily provide moral uplift and social value, a more basic justification for leisure emerged during the postwar era. The idea of fun for fun's sake and the shameless pursuit of pleasure played an increasingly important role in how free time was perceived and spent. It was a joy

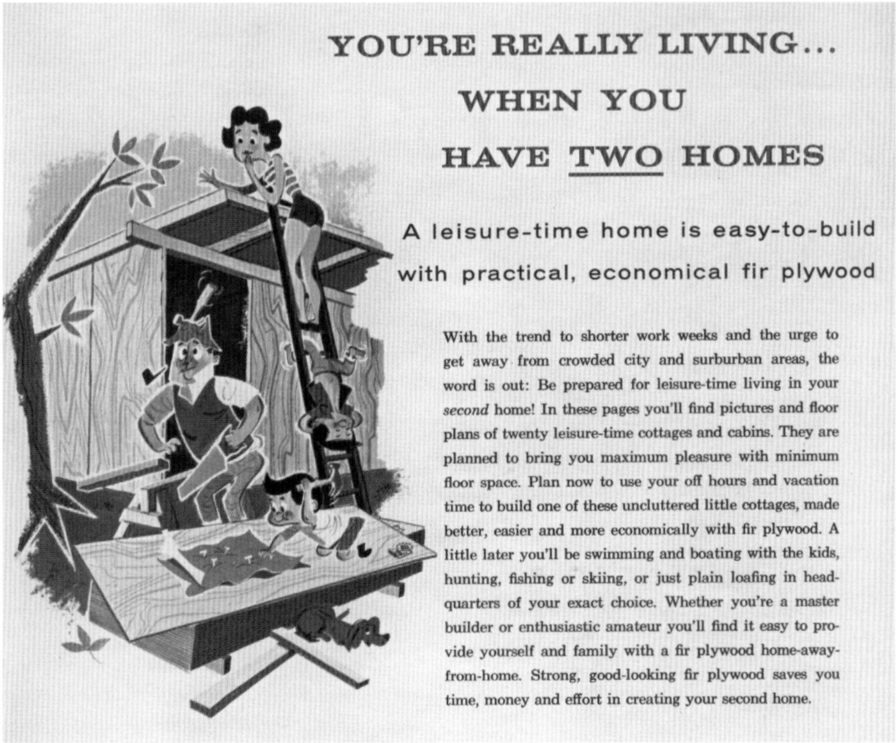

YOU'RE REALLY LIVING...
WHEN YOU
HAVE TWO HOMES

A leisure-time home is easy-to-build with practical, economical fir plywood

With the trend to shorter work weeks and the urge to get away from crowded city and surburban areas, the word is out: Be prepared for leisure-time living in your *second* home! In these pages you'll find pictures and floor plans of twenty leisure-time cottages and cabins. They are planned to bring you maximum pleasure with minimum floor space. Plan now to use your off hours and vacation time to build one of these uncluttered little cottages, made better, easier and more economically with fir plywood. A little later you'll be swimming and boating with the kids, hunting, fishing or skiing, or just plain loafing in headquarters of your exact choice. Whether you're a master builder or enthusiastic amateur you'll find it easy to provide yourself and family with a fir plywood home-away-from-home. Strong, good-looking fir plywood saves you time, money and effort in creating your second home.

From Douglas Fir Plywood Association vacation home plan book, 1958

rel chairs, to home renovations, additions, and construction. As more and more Americans became office workers—more adroit with the adding machine than the saw—hands-on projects provided a sense of fulfillment and accomplishment. With the cost of skilled tradespersons rising rabidly, doing it yourself was an economic imperative for those who wanted more than their salaries could cover.[24] Whether it was finishing an attic space or building a vacation home, couples, particularly young couples, saw do-it-yourself activities as a means of acquiring comforts that were increasingly considered necessities yet too expensive to purchase as finished products.[25]

In a culture still suffering from a Puritan hangover and for those still a little squeamish about leisure for leisure's sake, do-it-yourself projects were both productive and morally defensible. Those whose hobbies consisted of more work could not be considered lazy. Whether through construction or regular maintenance and repair, vacation homes offered the mix of leisure, labor, and self-affirmation that

Modest International Style beach houses, proposed by *Sunset* magazine, 1938

many Americans seemed to crave. (In fact, many articles pointed out that amateur vacation home builders got more work than they expected, as construction and upkeep left them more exhausted on Sunday night than they had been on Friday.)[26]

The aggressive marketing of electric tools, latex paints, linoleum, pressed-wood paneling, and prepackaged kits made home renovation and construction, seem within the capability of the hands-on hobbyist. With the intention of selling more plywood or other materials, companies developed booklets of second home plans, in which easy-to-build A-frame designs figured prominently. Others went a step further and formulated precut or prefabricated kits, which provided the customer with all the materials necessary to build a basic A-frame shell. Whether finishing a basement rec room or constructing an A-frame, do-it-yourselfers bought with sweat equity the middle-class necessities that they could not otherwise afford.[27]

POSTWAR ARCHITECTURE

In his book *Waiting for the Weekend*, Witold Rybczynski observed that "country retreats have always been an opportunity to break loose from the architectural constraints of the city."[28] While any building could serve as a getaway, unconventional designs furthered the fantasy of escape from the everyday world. Rustic "camps," for example, with bark exteriors and knotty furniture, had long allowed their wealthy owners to play pioneer in the Adirondacks. In the past those who could afford modest summer homes usually selected recognizable designs traditional to rural or mountainous settings: variations on the log cabin, English cottage, Cape Cod house, or bungalow. Except for log cabins, there was little difference between summer homes and permanent homes.[29]

The first designs to break with this convention were International Style beach houses dating to the late 1920s and 1930s. Built primarily on the east and west coasts, these modern structures, with featureless white walls, ribbon windows, flat roofs, and open interiors, were derived from a European industrial and socialist aesthetic that had nothing to do with leisure. Rudolph Schindler's concrete and glass Lovell Beach House, in Newport, California (1926), was one of the earliest done in the new form. It was followed by other designs on the California shore, as well as homes on Long Island by Warren Matthews, William Muschenheim, and the firm Peabody, Wilson and Brown.[30]

Five such homes appeared in a 1938 *Sunset* magazine plan book scattered among the typical cabin designs.[31] Though they resembled the much more elaborate and expensive custom-designed beach houses by Schindler and others, these homes offered basic avant-garde living at an affordable price. Where the log cabin was a bulwark against the wilderness, early modern vacation homes, with jutting terraces and copious plate glass, suggested a more engaged and salutary relationship with the outdoors. Nature was on display, more an accoutrement than a threat.

When the A-frame vacation home appeared in the early 1950s, it marked a new category of contemporary leisure architecture. This loose grouping mixed an up-to-date appreciation for active outdoor recreation with experimental tendencies ascendant in other areas of architectural design. The emphasis was on playful informality, dynamic structural concoctions, unconventional roof shapes, open plans, and unusual glazing configurations. Designers sought to produce dramatic structures with limited resources, goals that often proved complementary as tight budgets impelled innovation and modest size encouraged experimentation. The result was an accessible modernism, more likely found in the pages of *Better Homes and Gardens* and *Popular Mechanics* than in the "official" architectural press.

For those who found traditional vacation home styles a poor fit for contemporary ideas of leisure and who were equally unexcited by strict modernism, the A-frame and its whimsical offspring had great appeal. These homes were designed for and were a product of the postwar leisure culture. They were in tune with this era of outdoor living, of sun decks, breezeways, and the all-important deck and patio. They were uniquely suited for their function: the stylish, informal, active enjoyment of free time in natural surroundings. The magazine *Living for Young Homemakers* observed in 1961, "Vacation retreats are providing the ideal chance for designer and owner to unshackle all inhibitions. Fanciful expressions are popping up like bright impertinences against the conventional landscape. Houses and shelters are becoming more and more adventurous in themselves, inspired by shapes and forms that stir the imagination and invite the spirit to get away from it all."[32]

Playful roof forms set contemporary vacation homes apart from the by-then cliché flat-roofed structures and traditional year-round houses. It was a trend paralleled in postwar commercial, institutional, and civic architecture. New bank, car dealer, and restaurant

Plan companies and building material trade associations often promoted the new breed of contemporary vacation home forms. LEFT **The Sugar Pine, Western Wood Products Association, 1960;** CENTER **Design Number 717, Home Building Plan Service, 1965;** RIGHT **Three Stage Beach Cabin, Douglas Fir Plywood Association, 1964**

Frederick Liebhardt's vacation home for DFPA, 1958

Henrik Bull, Klaussen House, Squaw Valley, California, 1954

"How does he ever expect to be an architect if he can't invent a new roof?"

Alan Dunn cartoon in *Architectural Record*, September 1959

designs were replete with folded plates, hyperbolic paraboloids, cylindrical and spherical shells, bat wings, and saddles, often built in concrete or steel. Coming up with new versions seemed a rite of passage for aspiring architects. California's "coffee shop modern," or "Googie," architecture introduced a flamboyant vocabulary of cantilevered roofs, exposed trusses, and tilted glass walls that was part Frank Lloyd Wright organic, part *Jetsons* space age.[33] Expressionist designs, like Eero Saarinen's elegant TWA Terminal at New York's JFK Airport and the houses of John Lautner, left orthodox modernism behind, opening the door to playful engineering and symbolic, flexible forms.

Because plywood and two-by-sixes were the common material of modest contemporary vacation homes, their imaginative roofs were usually more angular, with intersecting planes rather than arches or domes. In an oft-copied design, architect Henrik Bull draped a pitched spent-wing roof over a large built-up ridgepole for his 1954 Squaw Valley house for Peter Klaussen.[34] Several years later Frederick Liebhardt came up with a Taliesin West knock-off for a plan book published by the Douglas Fir Plywood Association (DFPA).[35] In addition to distracting the eye from the usually basic square forms underneath, these roofs effectively spanned vacation home interiors with few or no partitions. By shedding or easily supporting heavy snow loads and with generous overhangs to block out bright sunlight, such designs also proved well suited to vacation area climates.

Essential in shaping the exterior appearance of the contemporary vacation home, unusual roof forms also helped define the interior. Structural beams, joists, and plank sheathing were left exposed in order to clearly articulate the roof shape on the inside. In many designs the angles and shifting pitches of the ceiling accentuated a living-room area open to the full height of the house. Kitchens and bathrooms were placed in the back, beneath upstairs loft bedrooms that were at least partially open to the living room below. Hallways were rare. Rooms opened into the living area, with Japanese shoji screens or curtains sometimes forming the only partition. A central tenet of modern architecture, open plans were especially suited to modest vacation homes. They allowed views through the glazed wall to be visible throughout the house, were more easily heated by a single fireplace, and lent a feeling of spaciousness to the small structures. They also emphasized the informality attendant to the postwar leisure life.

Venturesome leisure seekers interested in a contemporary vacation home could have one custom designed. Young architects were eager for the publicity that could accompany a provocative design. Popular magazines and plan books were a source for those who could not or chose not to hire an architect. Because the books and articles were aimed at a national audience with a range of preferences, even their "fresh," "interesting," and "unusual" homes were generally tamer than those done by architects as one-off commissions. *Woman's Day* counseled architects that all the vacation homes designed for the magazine "have had a strong element of the unusual without being crazy. They give the impression of being fun houses where the owner changes his personality and looses his tensions."[36] The Douglas Fir Plywood Association, a major vacation home promoter, described the type as "conservatively radical."[37]

Vacation home purveyors sought designs that were bold yet acceptable to middle-class Americans. Like the parties, getaways, and recreational activities that took place in and around them, contemporary vacation homes were relaxed, refreshing, and above all fun. To many, the A-frame best matched this description. Arriving in the early 1950s, it initiated a strain of vacation home design characterized by experimentation and informality. But affection for the A-frame was not instantaneous. It took almost a decade to bring the public around to the strange idea of a triangular vacation home. During this time the A-frame remained primarily a custom design, explored and refashioned by a succession of young architects. Through their well-publicized work, the postwar A-frame took shape.

Architect George Rockrise's self-designed vacation home, Squaw Creek, California, 1956

Chapter 3

Setting the Stage (1950–1957)
Architect Designed Custom A-frames

THIS FORM, SO FAMILIAR IN GEOMETRY,
OFFERED THE UNFAMILAR POSSIBILITY
OF DESIGNING A HOUSE WHOSE ROOF
ALSO FORMED THE SIDE WALLS.
— *ARCHITECTURAL RECORD*, 1950

By the early 1950s, economic, cultural, techno-logical, political, and demographic conditions were right for the emergence of new leisure-oriented architectural forms. Highways were turning wilderness into vacation areas, bank accounts were increasing, and work schedules were shrinking. A growing chorus of experts urged Americans to become involved in leisure pursuits for the sake of one's family and to use recreation time productively and wholesomely for the sake of the nation. As the decade progressed, a vacation home industry began to coalesce. It wasn't long before this new field found an appropriate symbol for the recreational attitudes that accompanied postwar prosperity: the A-frame, featured in countless magazine articles and cheaply replicated in prepackaged kits, seduced Americans with the promise of the good life.

The first phase of the A-frame boom (roughly 1950–1957) saw the introduction of the triangular form by a few young architects and designers, several of whom were immersed in the vibrant architectural atmosphere around San Francisco. They developed common ways of opening or enclosing gable ends, laying out interiors, orienting decks and entrances, and assembling, packaging, and marketing the A-frame. These treatments would appear again and again when the form began to achieve widespread popularity in the late 1950s.

It is not surprising that Northern Californians expressed an early interest in the A-frame. The region included burgeoning vacation destinations, such as Squaw Valley and Lake Tahoe, areas that were giving shape to the postwar leisure culture. It was home to the arbiter of the middle-class West Coast lifestyle, *Sunset* magazine. Most significant, San Francisco laid claim to its own regional aesthetic, variously called the Bay Area style, Bay Region modern, or Bay Area tradition. It was a loosely defined architectural attitude, marked by deference to site, open plans, a reliance on local natural materials, and a clear expression of

Wally Reemelin at work on his first A-frame, Berkeley, California, c. 1949

structure. The Bay Area style combined existing San Francisco traditions—based on designs by Bernard Maybeck, Julia Morgan, Ernest Coxhead, and others—with a select group of modernist priorities. It was an approach calibrated to the climate, topography, natural resources, and informal lifestyle of Northern California, one that translated readily into vacation home design.

Architect designed A-frames that came out of this period, even those built in the East, shared many Bay Area–style attributes. They successfully integrated contemporary functions and priorities with a form pulled from the vernacular past. Though avant-garde in their conceptual purity, they also featured comfortably familiar pitched roofs and cedar shingles. The use of exposed, unfinished wood and expanses of glass was clearly within the Bay Area vocabulary. The following A-frames were not the only ones built during the first half of the 1950s. Each example, however, distinguished itself by foreshadowing what was to come: the rise of the second home that through efficient design and modern materials and manufacturing, was affordable and attainable.

WALLY REEMELIN'S A-FRAME DUPLEX

In 1948 Wally Reemelin bought some land in the hills above Berkeley, California, at a public auction.[1] He paid about three hundred dollars each for several steeply sloped lots, intending to build some modest, inexpensive houses that could be rented to students. Trained in art and industrial design and a licensed mechanical engineer with a strong interest in architecture, Reemelin set out to develop a house that could fit on the sloped lots, could ride out earthquakes, and was small without feeling confined. He wanted to

demonstrate that "engineering principles applied to residential design could result in a structure that was sound, durable, economical, and interesting as well."[2] To best achieve these goals he designed an A-frame.

In late 1948 construction began on Reemelin's first triangular house, on Keith Avenue in Berkeley. The following spring, before work was completed on the first A-frame, he started three more. Two were considered a duplex in name, one further up the hill than the other; they were connected by a covered stairway, so that Reemelin could count them as a single structure and put them both on the same lot. In 1954 Reemelin built another A-frame next to the duplex, adding parking space beneath for three cars. It was followed over the next couple of years by a larger version—with two bedrooms and a bathroom upstairs—in the Oakland suburb Montclair and by one across from the Golden Gate Bridge, in Mill Valley.

Although each design was different, with dormers in different locations and small variations in the gable-end treatment, Reemelin's A-frames shared several attributes. They used a series of A-shaped trusses, with tie beams that divided the space into a lower level and an upper loft in the rear. These beams extended beyond the main rafters on one side, forming the roof of a main-level glazed dormer. The Douglas fir frames were bolted together and covered with two-inch tongue-and-groove sheathing; floor joists and cross-ties were doubled up for additional strength. After careful calculation, Reemelin spaced the A-frame trusses at wide, seven-foot intervals. This spare but sturdy structural arrangement minimized material costs, reinforced the impression of a simple design, and created a natural module by which to subdivide the interior.[3]

Wally Reemelin's first A-frame, under construction in Berkeley, 1948–49; BOTTOM LEFT Reemelin's wife and friends in front of the almost-completed A-frame

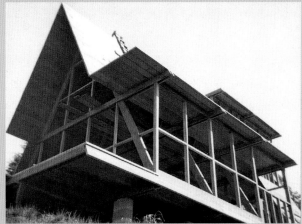

Reemelin's A-frame duplex, under construction, 1949

Reemelin's duplex, with the 1954 A-frame above

Reemelin's 1954 A-frame, built up the hill from the duplex, provided covered parking for three cars

The houses received considerable attention in local newspapers and even national publicity when one was featured in a 1950 issue of *Architectural Record*. They were modest structures, with a pleasing relationship between interior and exterior, and were located in the right topography, among steep hills and stunning ocean views; At the time, Reemelin didn't conceive of them as anything more than inexpensive housing, and so called them "Swiss chalets." It was only several years later, when the idea of the second home was on the rise, that Reemelin's A-frames were presented as vacation homes. In 1955 the *San Francisco Examiner* published an article in a special "Country Retreat" supplement of its Modern Living section. Titled "A Vacation Cabin—The Painless Way," the article called Reemelin's A-frame an affordable, easy-to-build rustic cabin, suitable for the first-time "do-it-yourselfer."[4]

JOHN CAMPBELL'S LEISURE HOUSE
During the fall of 1950, John Campbell sat down at his drafting table at the Campbell and Wong office in San Francisco to develop plans for a new vacation home.[5] He wanted to do something different, something that would stand out among the other submissions to *Interiors* magazine's annual collection of "Interiors to Come." He succeeded; the January 1951 article devoted two pages to his as yet unbuilt house. Shaped by his previous experience and the work of other Bay Area architects, Campbell's design was based on the equilateral triangle. Worked out with the help of Terry Tong, an office draftsman at the time, it was simple, devoid of ornament or frill, and almost monastic in its simplicity. It would become the most publicized A-frame of the decade, an affordable and attractive design that engendered more initial interest in the triangular form than any other.

The first project by Campbell and his professional partner, Worley Wong, to garner public attention was a vacation home at Fallen Leaf Lake, near Lake Tahoe. Built in 1947 from a steel, military-surplus Quonset hut, the design did little to alter the barrel-vaulted profile of the "Standard Quonset 20." A *Progressive Architecture* article

LEFT **John Campbell (lower center) and other members of the Campbell and Wong office, 1955;** RIGHT **Campbell and Wong Architects, Quonset Hut vacation home, Fallen Leaf Lake, California, c. 1947**

noted that "the designers [felt] very strongly about the undesirability of allowing anything like dormers with unorthodox roofs or other things unrelated in form or structure to project from and compete with the basic, continuous curved form of the Quonset."[6] The home could be easily expanded without disturbing the arched shape by placing additional structural ribs and corrugated skin at either end of the structure (just as A-frames would be expanded by inserting additional trusses). *Progressive Architecture* praised the fact that Campbell and Wong's design did not obscure the basic Quonset form, "which makes it almost impossible to point to something and say, 'Here is a wall,' and to something else and say, 'Here is a roof.'"[7] When the opportunity arose in 1950 to develop his vacation home for *Interiors* magazine, Campbell used the equilateral triangle to

exhibit a similar respect for simple forms and lack of distinction between wall and roof.

Illustrations accompanying the 1951 *Interiors* article showed a camplike setting with two separate A-frames on opposite corners of a hillside terrace. The text claimed that the houses could be fully furnished or equipped with only the bare necessities and that the sixteen-foot triangular trusses could be covered either with horizontal lap siding or "prepared boarding." In what later became a common refrain in the promotion of the A-frame as a do-it-yourself project, the article concluded, "Obviously, the process is within the brawn, energy and skill of normal young people."[8]

Campbell's design was open to interpretation. Initial renderings presented what would come to be called the Leisure House as a high-art minimalist-modernist design, a pair of fea-

TOP **The first Leisure House advertisement appeared in the** *San Francisco Chronicle*, **in November 1951** BOTTOM **Advertisement for Leisure House kit, 1952**

tureless planes converging to enclose an unpartitioned space. Unlike later A-frames that attempted to soften the austere angles with "gingerbread" eave boards and porches, the Leisure House reveled in its simplicity. The contemporary styling continued in the building's interior, which was shown in early drawings and models with Japanese and modernist furnishings. It was unquestionably sleek, sexy, and far removed from the typical vacation home. Yet there was no way of overlooking the fact that the Leisure House was essentially one big pitched roof. It was a hyperbolic expression of modernism's chief bugaboo. For many who had come to associate the flat roof with everything that was cold and impersonal about modernism, the shape of the Leisure House was reassuringly traditional. Like other Bay Area style designs, it warmed and lightened modernism by framing it in natural materials, emphasizing human scale, and asserting that architecture and fun need not be mutually exclusive.

A number of articles about the Leisure House quickly followed the initial "Interiors to Come" feature, including one in the California modernist magazine *Arts and Architecture*.[9] What really set the structure on the road to renown, however, was construction of a full-size model for the 1951 San Francisco Arts Festival.

Campbell presented the design in an almost sculptural form, using only a rough framework to indicate the door and window configuration. The front half of the house remained unenclosed, to function as a covered deck while a four-foot-wide gap on one side accommodated a "space-mural" especially designed for the exhibit.[10]

Almost immediately people began to contact the firm, asking about the A-frame. The clamor grew when, on the festival's closing day, a story about the design ran in the *San Francisco Chronicle*.[11] Campbell started offering copies of Leisure House plans for twenty-five dollars.[12] "Acclaim and outspoken interest on the part of the public and critics alike" led Campbell to quickly move to establish a prepackaged kit.[13] Working with a local construction company, he put together a package that included everything needed to build the basic house shell, from precut timber to nails and a hammer.

In early 1952 Campbell built his own Leisure House on a wooded hillside across from the Golden Gate Bridge in Mill Valley.[14] It was an awesome location that complemented the A-frame shape and appealed to the idyllic vacation home fan-

Leisure House exhibit at the San Francisco Arts Festival, 1951

tasies of potential buyers. Photographs of Campbell's personal Leisure House were used to promote the design for the next twenty years. As Campbell and friends completed construction of the Mill Valley house, he formalized plans for the precut kit and a network of franchises, while eventually spread at least as far as Los Angeles and Denver.[15] Promotional materials presented the package as a logical and economical choice for young families in search of their first second home. Jack and Helene Whelen of San Francisco were *Look* magazine's case study couple. Pictured sitting atop the stacked lumber that made up the kit, then assembling the trusses, and finally relaxing on the deck in front of the completed structure, they showed that "anyone who can lift a 2" x 6" could build the kit."[16] *Look*, with an enormous nationwide circulation of 3.7 million, was the first general interest magazine to publicize the Leisure House.[17] It must have been invaluable exposure for the nascent endeavor.

Interest in the Leisure House peaked in 1953. The San Francisco chapter of the American Institute of Architects gave it an honor award, and jurors Richard Neutra, Edward Durell Stone, and Pietro Belluschi called the design a "wonderful example of the weekend house."[18] It was featured again in the *San Francisco Chronicle*, *Arts and Architecture*, *Interiors*, and a *Sunset* vacation home book. A full-scale model was erected at a San Francisco department store's Vacation Carnival, where it shared the stage with a weight-lifting demonstration, a barbecue, a master gun engraver, a "swimsuit figure consultant," and, daily between 11 A.M. and 4 P.M., a TWA travel consultant, showing how to pack a suitcase.[19]

Over the next decade the Leisure House continued to appear in magazines, including *Sports Illustrated*, *True: The Man's Magazine*, and *The American Home*. It was featured in the United States pavilion at the 1958 Brussels World Exposition, alongside works by Edward Durell Stone and Mies van der Rohe. In his 1962 book *Vacation Houses*, author William Hennessey noted

Illustrations from a Leisure House franchise brochure, Los Angeles, c. 1953

John Campbell's Leisure House, Mill Valley, California, 1953

Leisure House, Mill Valley, California, 1953

**George Rockrise, Perlman House,
exterior and interior perspectives, c. 1954**

that "perhaps no Leisure House design had gained as much popularity as the A-frame during recent years. It is attractive to look at, easy to live in and inexpensive to build. Here is the granddaddy of them all, designed in 1950 by Campbell and Wong, San Francisco architects."[20]

Though Campbell continued to offer plans into the 1970s, there is little to suggest the extent and ultimate fate of the franchises or the total number of Leisure Houses built.[21] As the prominence of the Leisure House faded, it was replaced by innumerable variations designed by professional architects and backyard builders. The Leisure House marked a new phase in the history of the triangle-shaped structure. It was influential not so much for Campbell's interpretation of the A-frame but for his efforts at promotion and packaging. The savvy marketing and national exposure of the Leisure House would influence future designers and entrepreneurs and contribute significantly to the spread of the A-frame vacation home.

GEORGE T. ROCKRISE'S PERLMAN HOUSE

In the early 1950s David Perlman, a science writer for the *San Francisco Chronicle*, and his wife were just beginning to downhill ski. With three young children, they were interested in building a second home near the recently established ski resort at Squaw Valley. The Perlmans first signed a lease for a small plot of land offered by the United States Forest Service not far from the valley. The degree to which the area was still undeveloped in 1953 is indicated by the government's offer of such leases for free as long as the property was improved within a specified time. They met architect Joe Esherick, who was designing a home for Perlman's sister in Santa Cruz. Told that the Perlmans had only five thousand dollars to spend on the house, Esherick sketched out a simple A-frame over dinner.[22]

In the summer of 1953, with instructions from Esherick, the family headed to their new plot to measure and stake out the house. They quickly realized, however, that dense tree coverage above and below their land would obscure any view and further darken what they considered a "tunnel-like" design. The lot was also saturated with mosquitoes. Sobered but undeterred, the Perlmans gave up the Forest Service lease and purchased a sunny lot on the north slope of Squaw Valley. A short time later they met San Francisco architect George T. Rockrise at a party, where he mentioned that he had also purchased property in the valley. They hit it off, and Rockrise agreed to design the Perlman's house.[23]

Born in New York City to an English mother

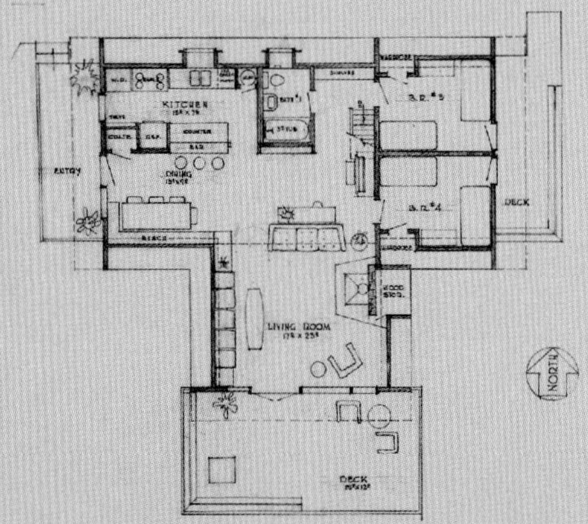

FIRST FLOOR PLAN ⅛" = 1'-0"

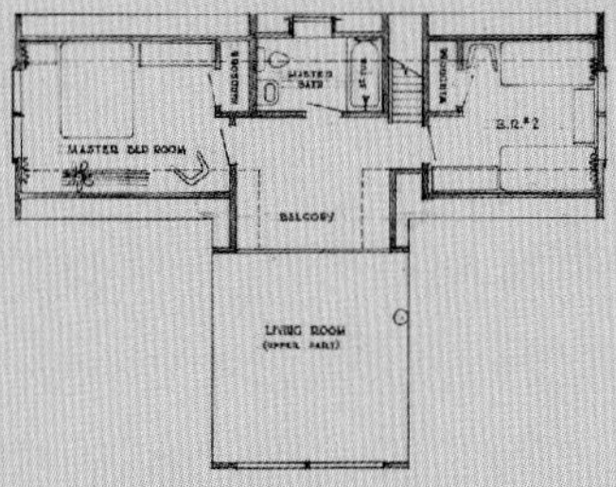

SECOND FLOOR PLAN ¼" = 1'-0"

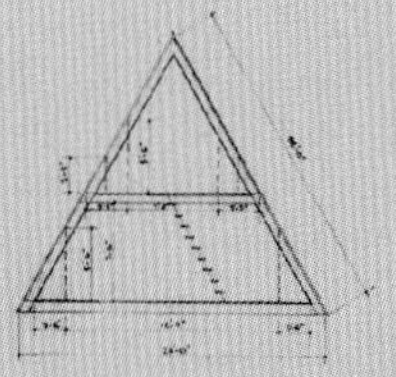

SECTION ¼" = 1'-0"

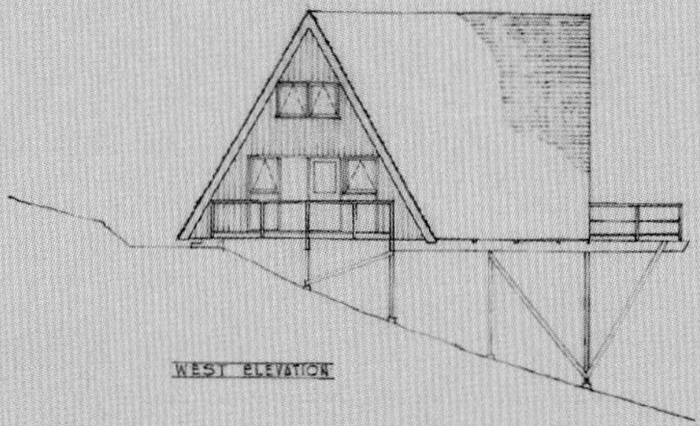

WEST ELEVATION

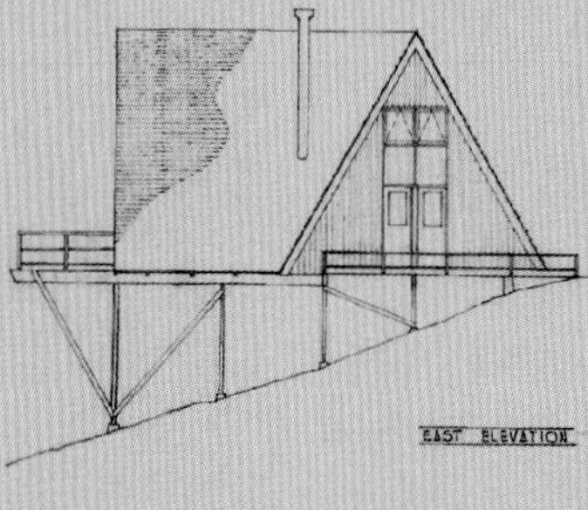

EAST ELEVATION

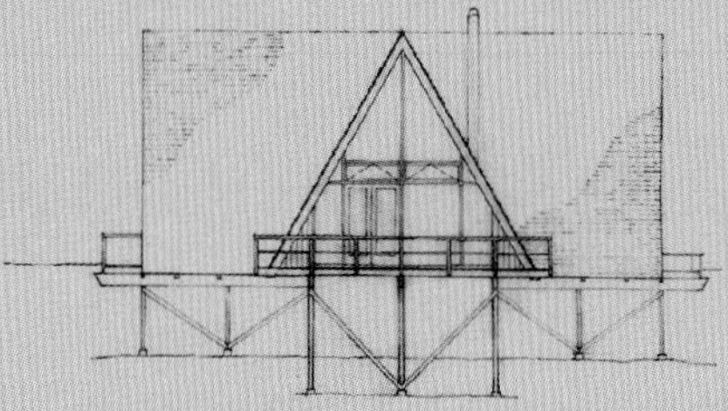

SOUTH ELEVATION

and a Japanese architect father, Rockrise studied design at Syracuse and Columbia. Following World War II, he worked with Edward Durell Stone on the El Pañama Hotel and with Gordon Bunshaft, Le Corbusier, and Oscar Niemeyer on the United Nations Headquarters. He relocated to San Francisco in 1947 and began a partnership with the well-known landscape architect Thomas Church before establishing his own office.

For the Perlman commission, Rockrise also began with the triangular scheme. He worked out a new interpretation using a model made from the cardboard packaging of a newly purchased dress shirt. One of the first designs to join two A-frame sections in a T-shaped plan, Rockrise's version allowed additional light to enter the interior and provided room for four bedrooms and two baths, thereby addressing the Perlmans' concerns about the potentially dark interior while meeting their needs for space and economy. These benefits were achieved without detracting from the basic A-frame shape. Inside, Rockrise's design included both "low-ceilinged coziness" beneath the loft areas and a "chapel-like vault [in] the main living room," all done with exposed fir beams and roof decking.[24] A glass gable end in the living room opened onto a large deck with dramatic views across the valley, where skiers could be seen tracing paths down powder-covered slopes.

The house was constructed during the summer of 1955; the large deck was used as a staging area for erecting the A-frames and completing the structure. Perlman hired a contractor who, new to the area and short on clients, agreed to build both the A-frame house and Rockrise's own residence for only ten dollars per square foot. When the Perlmans spent their first ski season in

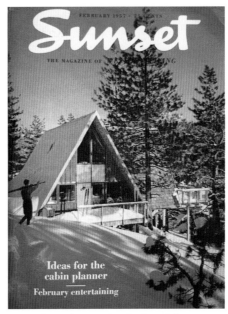

ABOVE *Sunset* **magazine featured George Rockrise's A-frame for David Perlman, February 1957;** OPPOSITE **Perlman House, preliminary elevations and plans, 1954**

the house that winter, there were fewer than twenty homes in Squaw Valley. Over time it would become one of America's premier leisure landscapes, host to a Winter Olympiad and a continual testing ground for the trials and errors of recreation architecture. Through it all the cross-gabled Perlman House stood, an unqualified success.

HENRIK BULL'S FLENDER A-FRAME
Although the postwar A-frame was born on the West Coast, Henrik Bull helped bring it east when he built what was probably the first A-frame in Stowe, Vermont, in the summer of 1953. Bull was a native of Stowe and studied under Buckminster Fuller at the Massachusetts

Perlman House, 1958

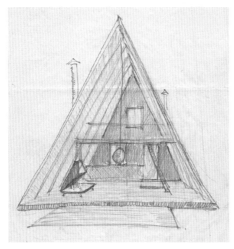

Institute of Technology (MIT). He was doodling one day during his last year at MIT when his roommate, John Flender, saw the drawing and half-jokingly proposed that they build it. Bull completed the sketches for a two-story A-frame with a gable end made entirely of glass, opening onto a cantilevered deck. Figuring that such a home would make their ski trips more affordable and that the design was simple enough to put together themselves, they became determined to see the project through. Though the original design was quite spartan, when Flender's brother and another couple signed on, the house plan was expanded to include indoor plumbing and an electric heating system.[25]

When they applied for a loan, though, they were told that even the more elaborate design was not enough to secure a mortgage. Like Reemelin and Campbell, Bull had originally designed his A-frame to rest on a pier foundation, one best adapted to a mountain site.

Unimpressed, the lenders were unwilling to finance a home that they considered a temporary structure. "No foundation, no mortgage" was the policy. Fifty years later John Flender acknowledged that the bankers did them a favor. The cinder block basement that Bull added fulfilled the lender's requirements and enhanced the livability of the design. By setting it into the hillside, Bull was able to incorporate the square foundation without affecting the geometric purity of the triangular shape above. It accommodated a simple bathroom, provided an unobtrusive location for utilities, and kept the upper levels less cluttered. Because the cellar was insulated, the pipes, pump, and water heater were all protected from freezing temperatures and did not need to be drained on Sunday nights before the return trip to Boston.

In the summer of 1953, with financing in order and a fifty-dollar half-acre of land midway between the village of Stowe and the ski slopes, construction got underway. The triangular trusses rested on two seven-hundred-pound, eight-by-ten-inch timber girders, which had been placed directly upon the cinder block foundation using a local tow truck derrik. Twenty-six feet long on each side, the triangular trusses were made from the longest new timber then available in Vermont.[26] Like most A-frames, the six trusses were put together on the ground and then hoisted into position, the first with a gin pole and the subsequent ones using a pulley attached to the trusses erected previous. Photographs of the process show the frames and their collar ties resembling a row of A's lined up on the Vermont hillside. After each truss was secured, work started on sheathing and shingling the roof, enclosing the gable ends, and finishing the interior. With the exception of excavating, pouring the cellar floor, and glazing the

Henrik Bull, Flender A-frame, interior and exterior sketches, 1953

ABOVE **Flender A-frame under construction, 1953; architect Henrik Bull (lower right)**
OPPOSITE **Flender A-frame interior, 1953**

south gable wall, all of the work was done by the owners and friends. Bull called it "Sunday carpentry and masonry."[27] Particularly good ski weather that first winter prevented the owners from finishing entirely until the following spring.

The interior was similar to that found in Reemelin's A-frame and the tens of thousands that followed. A full height living room was located in front of a loft bedroom over a kitchen in the rear. But it was the purity of form and dedication to proportion that set Bull's A-frame apart from many that followed. Particular care was devoted to a glazing scheme that complemented the triangular simplicity of the structure. Diagonal shadows cast by the window frame animated the geometry as they drifted across the exposed wood ceiling.

The A-frame partnership continued until the 1970s when each sold his share to John Flender (who still owned the house in 2003). The only significant alteration was the addition of a bedroom space alongside the original basement, necessary to accommodate Flender's growing family.

Henrik Bull ended up making a career of vacation home and recreation-oriented design. After finishing his studies at MIT, he moved to San Francisco and worked briefly for Mario Corbett, a well-known practitioner of the Bay Area style. His first private commission, in 1954, was a modest but striking vacation home for Peter Klaussen in Squaw Valley.[28] Applying lessons learned on the Flender A-frame, Bull developed a design vocabulary that included a loft overlooking a main living area, two-story windows that bathed the interior in sunlight and

directed views toward the landscape outside, and spaces that alternated between feelings of comforting enclosure and soaring openness.

Throughout the postwar era Bull continued to explore new approaches to leisure living, from a stripped-down plywood beach house for the Douglas Fir Plywood Association (DFPA) to a converted forty-thousand-gallon wine tank, all drawing inspiration from their respective sites and striving for a distinct yet affordable vacation home form. In the 1970s and 1980s he concentrated on resort condominiums. Today Bull's office, BSA, is among the best-known architectural firms that specialize in recreation design. Its work, including the Inn at Spanish Bay, the Visitor's Center at Point Reyes National

Seashore, and other vacation homes and resorts from Pebble Beach, Florida, to Keystone, Colorado, exhibit an enduring commitment to the Bay Area architectural sensibility: a preference for natural materials, a combination of tradition and innovation, and a clear understanding of how to make contemporary architecture a natural and unobtrusive extension of what are often stunning landscapes.

OPPOSITE **Flender A-frame with roof jacks still on from previous fall's shingling work, 1954;** ABOVE **Henrik Bull, Edwards House, a vacation home built from a wine barrel, Lake Tahoe, 1962**

ANDREW GELLER'S REESE HOUSE
Andrew Geller was educated at Cooper Union in New York City and, following World War II, worked in Raymond Loewy's office, where he developed designs for cameras, department stores, and prefabricated homes. In 1955 he designed his first vacation home, an A-frame in the Hamptons for Betty Reese. The house was featured in the *New York Times*, setting off a flood of requests for Geller vacation homes on sites throughout eastern Long Island. With these commissions, which he worked on in the late night and morning hours in his attic studio, Geller gained a reputation for developing unusual, almost sculptural vacation homes that bore little resemblance to any other building form.[29]

While his later designs grabbed considerable attention for their outlandish shapes, it was the 1955 A-frame for Betty Reese that launched Geller's career in vacation home architecture, proposed a new orientation for triangular struc-

tures, and helped boost the A-frame to national prominence. Reese was a Manhattan public relations pioneer, independent and unwilling to be confined to the role expected of women in the 1950s. When she set out to build a vacation home on the dunes of eastern Long Island, she wanted a design that reflected her individuality, allowed her to escape from the claustrophobia of her New York apartment, and, since her budget was only five thousand dollars, one that was cheap. Geller proposed an A-frame.[30]

By shifting the entrance from the gable end—customary on the A-frames discussed thus far—to the sloping sides and by running the building parallel to the shore, Geller emphasized the A-frame's longitudinal axis, blending it into the beach dunes. He cut into the triangle on the side facing the sea but left intact the cedar-shingled roof's angled profile to the rear. The beach side had two large picture windows, with awning sash below, that opened onto a deck

LEFT Andrew Geller; RIGHT Reese House interior sketch, 1955

running the length of the structure. Above, A-frame cross-ties extended beyond the triangular shape, doubling as joists for an upper level deck that itself doubled as a sunshade for the picture windows below. It was an ideal treatment for a beach setting, allowing in much more light than the typical A-frame while providing ample space for indoor and outdoor enjoyment of the setting and view.

Author Alastair Gordon called it "the most rudimentary sort of shelter, more a campsite than a formal house."[31] Like most of the early A-frames, the Reese House featured a simple interior. Framing and sheathing were left exposed. Furnishings were understated and functional: a couch along the wall facing the ocean, wicker chairs, reed mats, and a concrete block fireplace. Much of the interior was open to the full height of the structure, the exception being Reese's loft bedroom. This hideaway within a hideaway corresponded to the dormers seen on the exterior, opened onto the upper deck, and was reachable only via a retractable ladder.

Though conservative compared with many of the vacation homes that would later appear in the Hamptons, local building authorities originally took exception to the triangular scheme. Geller quelled criticism by assuring officials that the structure was similar to the potato barns that were once a fixture of the Long Island landscape. Like Schindler twenty years before, Geller passed the A-frame off as vernacular-inspired, traditional rather than radical or modern.[32]

When the Reese House appeared in the *New York Times* in 1957, it attracted considerable attention. Thinking it was a model home, a wave of interested leisure seekers swept into Southampton to see it for themselves. One, Leonard Frisbie, was so taken with the house that he insisted Geller design an identical one for him in Amagansett, Long Island. Unwilling to repeat himself exactly, Geller simply reversed the floor plan. By the early 1960s, Geller had made a second career designing vacation homes.

He became one of the architects of choice for the New York and New England profession-

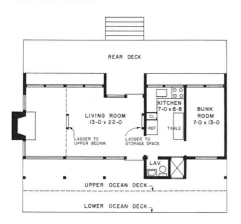

LEFT **Reese House, plan;** RIGHT **Betty Reese in front of her A-frame, Sagaponack, Long Island, 1955**

Reese House view from the beach; OPPOSITE **view toward kitchen and bunkroom**

Reese House, from the beach

Pearlroth House, Westhampton, Long Island, 1959

Elkin House, Amagansett, Long Island, 1966

als looking for their own slice of the postwar leisure life. Based partly on solutions developed for the Reese House, many of Geller's later commissions were visually striking yet minimalist in their materials and appointments. Assemblies of bow-sided block shapes with slanting walls and unusual window placements or cubes tipped on edge as if to mock the pure modernist box were typical of Geller's style. The architect explained that "of all the forms of dwelling place, none allows so much room for fun as a summer house. Furnaces and carports and laundry rooms are left behind in the city, and the elements one works with are sunlight and space."[33] Unconventional structural forms were carried inside, where open plans reflected the exterior shapes. Arranged around central living areas

that featured full-height windows aimed at the view, the interiors revealed the simple construction of two-by-six framing and plank sheathing. Geller's designs were unusual but thoroughly functional; they accommodated beach life and provided a reinvigorating, informal environment for their owners.

The homes designed by Reemelin, Campbell, Bull, Rockrise, and Geller laid the groundwork for the A-frame's ascent. Those first years, between Reemelin's 1949 Berkeley duplex and the 1955 article on Geller in the *New York Times*, were ones in which both the conventions of A-frame style and the typical variations were established. Innovations and developments were still to come, of course, but the vast majority of A-frames that were built in the period that

Christmas card Betty Reese sent to Andrew Geller, illustrated by Alan Dunn

followed owed much to these early designs.

During the postwar era, Americans wanted to live the California dream of hip leisure, ensconced in butterfly chairs and resting on tatami mats. Walter Reemelin, John Campbell, and George Rockrise were there to accommodate postwar leisure seekers with a vision of triangular living. Joined by Henrik Bull in Stowe, Vermont, and Andrew Geller on Long Island, these architects shared a desire to merge nature and design, quality and affordability, inside and outside, relaxation and vigor. Their solution was the A-frame vacation home.

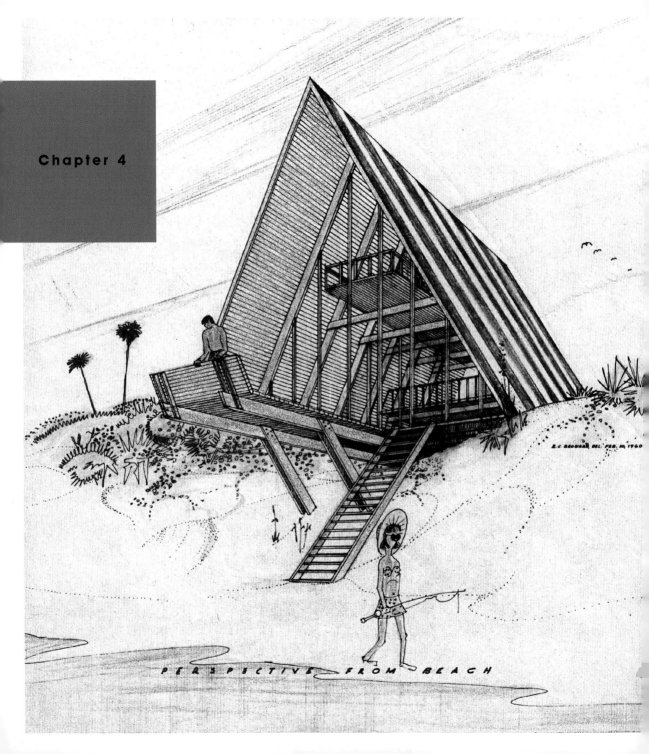

Chapter 4

PERSPECTIVE FROM BEACH

Popularity, Plan Books, and Promotion (1958–1962)

ALMOST EVERYONE IS INTRIGUED BY
THE A-FRAME DESIGN, SO POPULAR IN
TODAY'S VACATION HOME.
—*AMERICAN HOME MAGAZINE*, 1961

By the early 1960s, the benefits of the postwar consumer economy lifted millions of American families into the middle class. Having purchased their first home in the suburbs, many now set their sights on a vacation home, a place to escape and live the leisure lifestyle. No longer limited to Northern California and pockets in the East, the A-frame became a national phenomenon. Its popularity was encouraged by timber companies and building product manufacturers, plan book publishers and magazine editors who vigorously promoted the A-frame as an affordable, acceptably modern vacation home option.

While some saw the A-frame as just a fashionable trend, more provocative than practical, there were pragmatic reasons for its appeal. The A-frame was cheap and easy to build by the professional and hobbyist alike.

Appropriate in a variety of locations, it was altered, expanded, reconfigured, or stripped down to match almost any budget or desired use. It could be an austere hunting lodge, sheltering little more than a cot and fireplace, or a luxurious weekend retreat, rivaling most year-round homes in size and appointments. To some, the A-frame was a locus for entertaining, to others a hermitage. At a time when the emphasis was on low-cost designs that "stirred the imagination," the A-frame delivered both. It was a dramatic means of enclosing the most space with the least amount of money, material, and manpower. No other building form could reasonably marry a six-hundred-square-foot floor plan with twenty-foot-high ceilings. The triangular shape had its limitations, but for the price and effort no other vacation home form equaled the A-frame's allure.

Robert C. Broward, perspective drawing of Robert Walker House, Ponte Vedra Beach, Florida

78

AT HOME ANYWHERE

In 1952 the *San Francisco Chronicle* noted that, with modifications, John Campbell's Leisure House could "make a fine ski shelter, a beach house, a mountain cabin or well-equipped week-end retreat." Illustrations showing an open version of the house decked out as a cabana or a snow-covered ski hut enclosed by diagonal wood paneling, reinforced the claim.[1] Owners across the country found that the triangular structure matched their local climate and topography. By 1969, a United States Department of Agriculture (USDA) publication noted that "the A-frame cabin, a very popular type of recreational second home throughout the United States, had been built by many people in mountain areas, at the shore from Maine to Florida, and across the country."[2] Whether western mountainside or sandy New England shore, the site was suitable for the A-frame. Log cabins were out of place on the beach, and modern glass boxes did not really work in snow country. But the A-frame had no such constraints. To many, the triangular shape reflected mountain peaks and pine trees and thus was particularly fitting in an alpine environment. Others considered the triangular

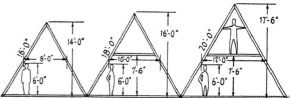

A-frames came in all sizes; these three, from Sunset's 1963 book *Cabins and Vacation Houses*, were relatively modest.

shape "a conversation piece even in sunny or tropical vacation lands," where it mirrored the dunes or steep slopes of nearby cliffs.[3]

The equilateral truss, upon which most A-frames were based, is one of the strongest forms of construction. In fact, the triangular vacation home's strength was legendary. Stories abound of A-frames surviving against the odds, shaken but not destroyed by tornados or withstanding weighty loads of snowfall. Mudslides pushed Wally Reemelin's first Berkeley A-frame five feet off its foundation, with no resulting structural damage. Architect Robert Broward's A-frame at Ponte Vedra, Florida, was one of the only buildings on a mile-long stretch of beach to weather Hurricane Dora in 1964. Perhaps the most dramatic survival tale is of Blair and Joyce Barner's A-frame on Spirit Lake Highway about sixteen miles from Mount St. Helens. The family was just a few days away from finishing construction when the volcano erupted in May 1980, in Oregon. It was the nearest house to the mountain still standing after the initial earthquake, the lateral blast, and the subsequent mud and ash flows. When it was over, the Barner's vacation home sat beneath four and a half feet of ash, mud, and debris. Forbidden from rebuilding in what was designated a "red zone," the family

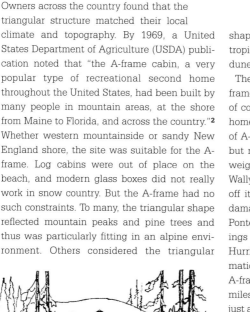

John Campbell's Leisure House as ski cabin

STRENGTH:

Your Alpine Villages A-Frame is really not an A-Frame! It is actually a series of rigid triangular sections tied together into a single indestructible unit that defies high winds and heavy snow loads. (See diagrams)

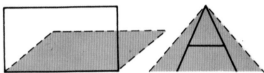 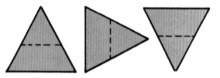

Conventional construction — needs bracing and other supplementary support.

Conventional A-Frame structure — legs are only spiked to the floor structure, have a tendency to spread and collapse.

BUT . . .
NO MATTER HOW YOU LOOK AT IT — The ALPINE VILLAGES triangular-framed ALPAN Home, a rigid locked equilateral triangle, cannot spread, sag, or collapse; and it is further stiffened by the addition of collar ties for upper deck support.

TOP From a prefabricated A-frame sales brochure, c. 1962; BOTTOM LEFT **Barner A-frame before the eruption of Mount St. Helens, Spirit Lake Highway, Oregon, 1980;** BOTTOM RIGHT **After the eruption, 1980**

ABOVE **Pilings, whether concrete or wood, provided a cheap support for A-frames on the beach or in the mountains;** OPPOSITE **A timber trade association placed this series of step-by-step diagrams, tauting easy A-frame construction in a 1961 issue of** *Popular Science*

partially excavated the house and opened the "Buried A-frame" tourist attraction.[4]

Its light weight and simple rectangular footprint made the triangular vacation home amenable to virtually any sort of foundation. If it was destined for a shoreline or flat lot, concrete blocks atop concrete footings often sufficed. More substantial A-frame designs or those seeking a more secure purchase could be placed on a concrete slab. Later versions were often built over fully excavated poured concrete basements, which provided a storage space or habitable lower level. A series of poured concrete or timber piers driven into the ground was another inexpensive alternative. *Field and Stream* observed that "the pier-type foundation is highly practical for either a lake or seaside location, where protection from high tides and flooding is

a consideration, or in mountainous country, where it is necessary to adapt the layout to an uneven lot."[5] Wood pilings could be driven straight down—like the Reese House—or, as in the 1964 A-frame designed by Robert Broward, they could be set at an angle, a continuation of the diagonal rafters, emerging from a sandy landscape.

CHEAP AND EASY

The A-frame's low cost and ease of assembly contributed enormously to its popularity. The more affordable the design, the more families, many of whom had just arrived in the ranks of the middle class, could consider its purchase. Those selling A-frame plans, and later A-frame kits, worked to keep them cheap, no more expensive than the price of a new car in some

Why an A-frame goes up so fast

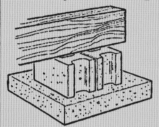

SIMPLE FOUNDATION requires only a few main beams supported on concrete-block piers. The blocks, usually two side by side, rest on concrete footings that go below the frost line.

A-FRAMES CAN BE PREFABBED on the ground unless very heavy beams are used. Each completed frame then serves as a pattern to insure fast and accurate alignment of next one.

TWO EASY WAYS to get strong, interlocking joints: At left, single wall beams are straddled by doubled floor beams. At right, doubled wall beams straddle a single floor beam.

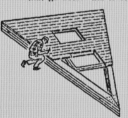

END GABLES can also be pre-assembled, complete with siding and door and window openings. This makes it easy to frame openings accurately without climbing around in mid-air.

FRAMES ARE HOISTED UP one at a time and held temporarily in place by diagonal braces. Two persons with a third helper pulling on a line can raise all but the heaviest A-frames.

WITH FRAMES IN PLACE, exterior panels or siding are nailed on to complete the shell in as little as six hours. Temporary cleats nailed to roof let you walk up the steep sides

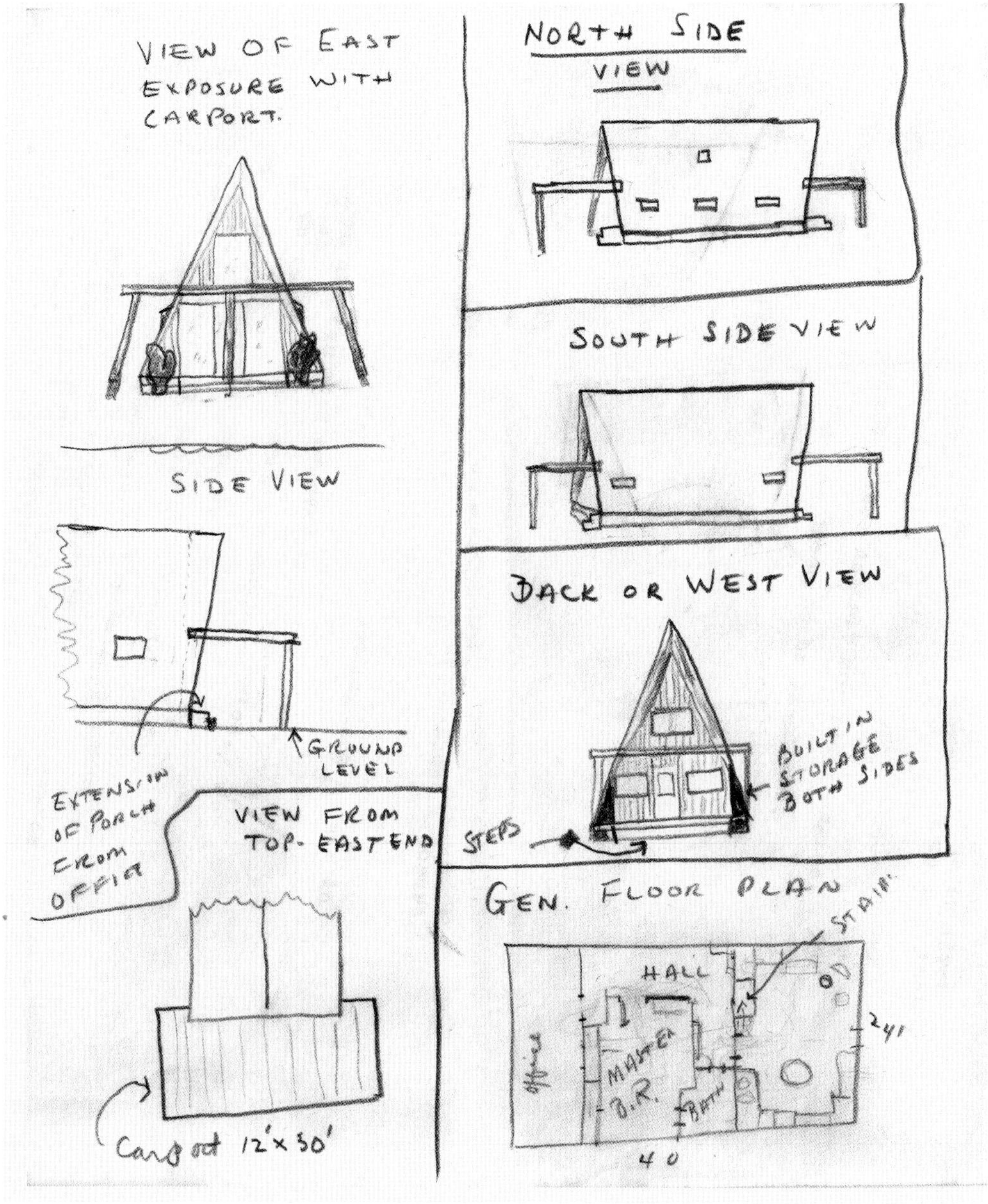

VIEW OF EAST EXPOSURE WITH CARPORT.

NORTH SIDE VIEW

SIDE VIEW

SOUTH SIDE VIEW

BACK OR WEST VIEW

EXTENSION OF PORCH FROM OFFICE

GROUND LEVEL

BUILT IN STORAGE BOTH SIDES

STEPS

VIEW FROM TOP- EASTEND

GEN. FLOOR PLAN

STAIR

HALL

Office

MASTER B.R.

BATH

241

40

Carport 12'x50'

cases. Considerable savings of both time and money resulted from the house's modular design (modular in that its easily replicated trusses were identical in shape and dimension). Costs were also kept down by skipping insulation. Even those built as ski lodges often had no more than plywood, building paper, and perhaps shingles between the interior and the cold outside.

The materials typically used to construct postwar A-frames also contributed to their reasonable price. From Rudolph Schindler's reliance on plywood in the Bennati House to plan book designs with pressed-wood panels and laminated sheathing, the modest A-frame proved well suited to a new breed of lightweight manufactured materials. It was characteristic of a general shift in vacation home construction that had begun before World War II. In 1961 the author of a popular vacation home guidebook observed that "despite the strong favor toward rugged, substantial cabin effects, we have in recent years come almost suddenly into an era when the basic concept of lightness rather than weight and ruggedness in construction is rapidly occupying an imposing place in the building of small cabins."[6] Designers, looking to shave costs and simplify construction, turned increasingly to lightweight materials and simple construction methods.

Plywood, Masonite, Formica, and Homasote panels lowered material and labor costs, as well as the skill level required for construction. Where shingles or lap siding was considered extravagant, designers often called for marine-grade plywood for both interior partitions and exterior cladding. Plylumber Siding, a product developed by Potlatch to resemble cedar shakes on the outside and "rustic wood paneling" on the interior surface, provided textural variation and the illusion of a more substantial roof com-

position.[7] Texture One-Eleven (T1-11), a grooved plywood panel, was used along the gable ends and dormers of some A-frames to resemble reverse board-and-batten siding.

As everyone pointed out, the A-frame was an easy structure to build. If the design was the typical equilateral triangle, with three sixty-degree angles, the dimensions of each truss were identical. Both the triangular frames and the gable ends could be assembled first and then hoisted into an upright position. One article, which attributed much of the A-frame's popularity to its ease of construction, noted that "you can assemble all the frames for the cabin right on the ground and put them up in one operation. A good-size cabin may have as few as four or five frames, connected only by the siding you stretch across them. Tricky gable-roof framing is eliminated."[8] When designed around the four-by-eight-foot dimensions of a sheet of plywood, the triangular homes could be built with less material, with less cutting, and by less skilled hands. With glass gable ends and a predominant roof, there was little wall space to paint. In fact, some suggested not painting at all, leaving the wood "unfinished to weather to the glistening caste of driftwood."[9] All of these factors made the A-frame more attractive to do-it-yourselfers and low-budget builders, professional and amateur.

POPULAR, DESPITE ITS FLAWS

The A-frame's popularity is particularly impressive when one considers that it came about despite inherent and obvious flaws in its form. Simplicity, a dramatic shape, ease of construction, and low cost imposed certain limitations, some of which were hard to avoid without losing the triangular look. The main liabilities of a basic A-frame were a lack of space in the lower

Roger Bowman's amateur sketches for a home and motel office show how the A-frames simplicity encouraged amateurs to customize their own design.

corners, heating and cooling difficulties, and a dark interior.

Because the A-frame was all roof and because that roof began to pitch inward at floor level, a certain amount of space was lost, or at least of limited use, between the floor and the point where a person could stand upright. The problem was similar to that faced by a boat owner below deck, only in reverse. Guidebooks suggested that these pockets were best utilized for wiring, pipes, and storage, a place to stash food, LPs, or skis. Some owners, especially of the smaller A-frames, just got used to living close to the floor, spread out on rugs, tatami mats, or pillows. Modern furniture, low and thin-cushioned, helped somewhat, as did the new prefab fireplaces, which could be tucked into lower corners. Sloping walls were most problematic in the bathroom and kitchen, where a two-foot-deep countertop set at waist level actually took up twice that amount along the floor. Lost space was less of an issue on upper levels, where beds were placed directly against the walls, parallel to the length of the house.

The full-height living room and loft configuration typical of A-frames was brighter and felt more spacious and informal than a more divided plan; it was also notoriously difficult to heat and cool evenly. In the summer the large roof area and glass gable wall cooked the air inside. Trapped beneath the cathedral ceiling, this warm air made the upper level a stuffy and uncomfortable place to sleep. Winter weather was equally trying. Heated air hovered immediately beneath the roof peak, leaving the loft bedrooms cozy, the main floor chilly, and heating equipment and fireplaces overburdened. Of little consequence in the fifties and early sixties when fuel oil was cheap, A-frame climate control became an

increasingly crucial liability when gas prices rose and the 1970s energy crisis hit.

A third drawback to basic A-frame designs, and the one that early on prompted departure from the pure triangular shape, was the lack of natural light in the interior. A *Sunset* vacation home guide remarked that "intense light from end walls almost always has to be balanced with light from the center, or else the center of the building tends to be gloomily dark."[10] Despite the suggestion, most designers avoided placing windows on the angled roof wall, where rain or melting snow would inevitably find its way inside.

But there were ways around the flaws. Since designers first adopted the A-frame for use as a vacation home, they introduced modifications intended to correct the lack of light and the inefficiencies in space and heating and cooling. The goal was to increase the quality of A-frame

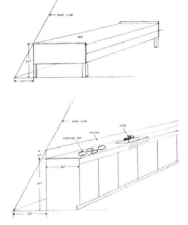

Drawings by Paul Corey in his 1967 book *Holiday Homes,* **showing space lost to the typical sloping A-frame roof**

living without losing the distinct triangular shape and its structural benefits. The A-frame offered great flexibility, and designers responded with ingenuity.

Dormers were the most common means of both rationalizing interior space and increasing the availability of natural light. When added to the ground floor, they accommodated sliding glass doors, window walls, or a kitchen setup closer to that found in conventional structures. Usually structural cross-ties were carried beyond the main roof to form the dormer's flat roof. On the upper level dormers provided a vertical surface for windows that were much less vulnerable to moisture than windows set directly into the sloping roof plane. Whether on the upper or lower level, dormers increased usable floor space by opening up right-angled corners and increasing headroom where it was most needed. Depending on the extent of the dormer treatment, they could be an inconspicuous or central design element. An alternative to boxing out portions of the triangle was insetting a vertical wall within the rows of trusses. Schindler's Bennati House and Geller's Reese House demonstrate how inset glazed walls provided increased daylight and more flexible plans. When the angled rafters were continued down to the floor level, the essential equilateral form was retained. The drawback, of course, was a further reduction of usable interior space.

Dormers and inset walls were a way to subtly vary the basic A-frame. More radical was a juxtaposition of additional gables. T-shaped versions, like George Rockrise's house for David Perlman, were quickly followed by X, Y, and L shapes and even more elaborate configurations, all designed to increase natural light, expand interior space, and retain a dramatic formal statement.

85

LEFT **Loft bedrooms could be stifling in the summer and stuffy in the winter;** RIGHT **A large kitchen by A-frame standards; without a dormer, counter space and headroom were limited**

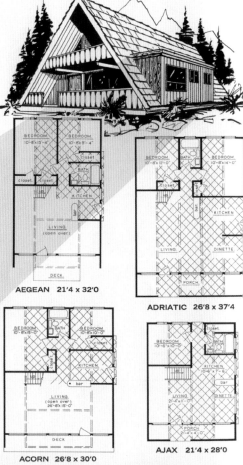

AEGEAN 21'4 x 32'0

ADRIATIC 26'8 x 37'4

ACORN 26'8 x 30'0

AJAX 21'4 x 28'0

THE MODIFIED "A" FRAME

Often referred to as the "optimum design," the modified A-frame retains the aesthetic appearance of an A-frame and yet offers that "open" feeling found in more conventional styled homes. Modified sections can be added on either or both sides, thus creating loads of vertical wall space without destroying the desirable exterior appearance of the A-frame.

"Modified" A-frame with dormer, providing additional light and space to the kitchen area, Lindal Cedar Homes, 1967

Flexibility, simplicity, affordability, and novelty somewhat explain the A-frame vacation home boom; but it could not have happened without the active involvement of boosters in the building and publishing industries who latched onto the rising interest in A-frames and used it to further sales. Building supply and timber companies capitalized on the concept's increasing popularity with the publication of A-frame designs featuring their materials. A-frames were the cover girls and centerfolds of vacation home plan books, which appeared with increasing frequency in the early 1960s. Mass-market magazines like *Popular Mechanics*, *American Home*, *Woman's Day*, *House Beautiful*, and *Mechanix Illustrated* made sure to include triangular designs in their coverage of the vacation home market, further propelling the A-frame toward its peak in the years ahead.

DR. HELLYER AND THE DFPA

In the spring of 1958 the DFPA sponsored a ten-page plan book titled *Leisure-Time Homes of Fir Plywood*. Urging customers to "plan now to use [their] off hours and vacation time to build one of these uncluttered little cottages, made better, easier and more economically with fir plywood,"

Exterior and interior photographs of multiple-gable A-frame by John Terrence Kelly, c. 1962

88

**Cover of DFPA plan
book, 1958**

the book featured plans for six vacation homes, as well as suggestions for plywood boats, boathouses, and outdoor furniture.[11] Based in Tacoma, Washington, the DFPA was established in the 1930s to further plywood manufacturing technology and the use of plywood products. W. E. Difford, managing director of the association in the 1950s, saw financial promise in the emerging leisure market and so set off to encourage new vacation home construction as well as the amount of plywood used in that construction.[12]

Advertisements for *Leisure-Time Homes* prominently featured the plan book's one A-frame, designed by a Tacoma pediatrician, Dr. David Hellyer.[13] A very modest triangular vacation home, with plywood shingles and inset vertical walls on both upper and lower levels, Hellyer's design was an immediate attention getter. Within a few months of publication, the DFPA had filled twelve thousand orders for Hellyer's plan.[14] A year later the association had received seventy thousand requests for information on the vacation homes offered in its plan book.[15] The overwhelming response to *Leisure-Time Homes* confirmed Difford's intuition about the vacation-home market's potential. The widespread interest in Hellyer's design hinted at the A-frame boom that lay ahead.

Raised in Japan, Switzerland, England, and Southern California, Hellyer was a twentieth-century Renaissance man. He authored several books, including a well-known volume on child rearing, cofounded a ski lift company, and established a wildlife refuge and education center near his home, outside Olympia, Washington. Though not formally trained in architecture, Hellyer came up with a well-proportioned, nicely detailed, spare version of the A-frame, one that remained an important component of the DFPA's vacation home initiative for the next twenty years.

Hellyer's design differed in several ways from those that preceded and followed it. Most A-frames at that time were built with a series of identical triangular trusses, but Hellyer used only two principal trusses, one at either end, with rafters set between. This allowed both floors to open from the inset walls onto decks unobstructed by angled rafters. By projecting the end rafters two feet above the roof ridge, Hellyer offered a playful reference to both tepee poles and Japanese cross-bladed rafters. The relationship between the first and second floors also distinguished Hellyer's design from the typical A-frame. Instead of a full-height living area and second floor loft, he extended the second floor the entire length of the house, creating two distinct living areas. Originally, the only means of reaching the second level was by way of an exterior ladder and a door.

Hellyer's friend Tom Sias, then the DFPA's public relations director, tipped his employer off to the design. After reviewing the project, the association offered to provide all of the plywood necessary to construct the house in exchange for the unrestricted use of the plans. Hellyer first erected the A-frame, minus windows and fixtures, in the yard behind his permanent home, near Tacoma. Satisfied that the scheme was viable, he disassembled it and floated it across Puget Sound to the building site at Henderson Inlet near Olympia. The structure was then re-erected in a single day with the help of several friends while a DFPA-hired photographer documented the process.[16]

The DFPA was attracted to Hellyer's A-frame for obvious reasons. Here was its material prominently displayed and central to the design of a cheap, increasingly popular vacation house form. Exterior grade plywood sheets functioned as both interior and exterior sheathing, providing lateral rigidity and a smooth contemporary

A-FRAME BEACH CABIN

Dr. David T. Hellyer, *Designer-Owner*

If you want a second home that's strikingly different, try this double-deck A-Frame style. Although the A-Frame has been used for many types of storage and shelters (its origins are in antiquity) this design represents one of its latter-day applications to a dwelling. The structure rests on king-sized base beams supported by nine concrete pilings. The roof of full-size Exterior fir plywood panel "shingles" act as both exterior and interior covering. Properly edge-butted and nailed, the strong, durable plywood panels provide the lateral rigidity that's needed with this type of frame. Texture One-Eleven "grooved" Exterior plywood side sections were nailed-up at owner's town home during the winter for assembly during warm weather on the building site. Two top-deck bedrooms are reached by outside stairway. Porch, living room, built-in kitchen and bathroom fill the first deck. Roof panels and siding were left unfinished to weather to the glistening caste of driftwood.

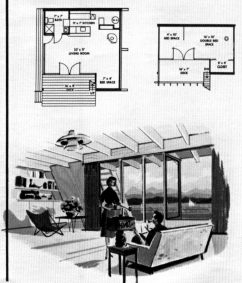

NEW full-color booklet shows 20 easy-to-build fir plywood cabins

HERE'S the perfect source of ideas for anyone planning to build a vacation cabin. Smart, modern designs by leading architects for cabins of every type and size, complete with pictures in natural settings, floor plans and building tips. Plans call for simple, straightforward construction with light, strong fir plywood to save you time, money and trouble when you build.

complete plans available for all 20 cabins

MAIL THIS COUPON TODAY FOR HELPFUL CABIN IDEA BOOKLET

DOUGLAS FIR PLYWOOD ASSOCIATION
Dept. 19, Tacoma, Wn. (Offer good USA only)

Please send me "Leisure-time Homes of Fir Plywood." I enclose 10c to cover mailing.

Name

Address

City................Zone.......State

**LEFT Dr. David Hellyer's A-frame beach cabin in *Leisure-Time Homes of Fir Plywood*, 1958
RIGHT DFPA advertisement, 1958**

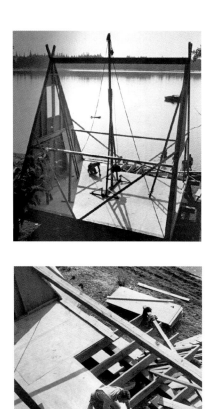

ABOVE **The completed Hellyer A-frame, 1957**

OPPOSITE **Promotional photos of the Hellyer A-frame under construction, Henderson Inlet, Washington, 1957**

INSIDE AND OUT,
PLYWOOD BUILDS A BETTER LEISURE-TIME HOME.

Plywood roof sheathing is a superior base for all types of finish roofing. Holds nails well, adds strength and performance.

Plywood ceiling paneling is easy to install and finish. Apply panels full size or in interesting patters with variety of surface textures available.

Exterior plywood is perfect for covering undersides of eaves...eliminating distracting joints and visible rafters. Always interesting, eye-appealing.

Exterior plywood does yeoman service outside the cabin, too, in striking fences and windbreaks to provide privacy or shelter from sun and wind.

Plywood cabinets are easily customized to meet your exact needs...show the real beauty of real wood or provide a perfect base for any painted finish.

Clean-lined Exterior plywood siding is easy to install. May be applied as wide-lapped siding, board-and-batten or flat panel.

Plywood provides firm, solid crack-proof backing for bathroom tile or other special interior wall surfaces.

Rich-looking but economical plywood wall paneling glows with the soft warmth of real wood.

Plywood subfloors and underlayment add strength and rigidity.

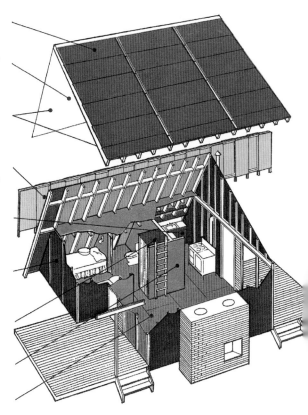

finish. No shakes or other roofing materials were used. Rather, the panels were laid lengthwise with their edges overlapping like giant shingles; the rear facade alone used nineteen four-by-eight-foot sheets. Texture One-Eleven grooved plywood panels covered the gable end walls and the vertical inset walls, where they continued the grooved pattern on the plank deck.[17]

Plans in *Leisure-Time Homes* cost twenty-five cents each. All of the designs were a departure from traditional vacation home design. The predominance of plywood and its four-foot module gave the designs a stripped down, angular appearance that emphasized smooth surfaces broken only by battens covering the panel joints. With shapes ranging from the barnlike gambrel to gently sloping sheds, the rooflines were particularly unusual; none more so than Hellyer's A-frame, which the booklet called "strikingly different."[18]

Over the next decade Hellyer's A-frame was featured in such varied publications as the *New York Times*, *Popular Mechanics*, the National Association of Home Builders (NAHB) *Journal of Homebuilding*, the American Automobile Association's *American Tourist*, *Medical Economics*, and half a dozen how-to vacation home books. The NAHB article noted that the house was "designed for the Douglas Fir Plywood Association, pioneer of new uses for the A-frame."[19] Six years after its initial publication Hellyer's A-frame tied with a design by George Matsumoto for the most often requested plan among the twenty-two offered by the DFPA.[20] During the 1960s the DFPA (later renamed the American Plywood Association) furthered its involvement in the vacation home market. The association released an expanded set of vacation home plans, featuring an additional A-frame called the Ranger; hosted a

WWPA advertisements featured A-frames as late as 1969

national vacation home conference; produced a series of guides for builders and developers interested in the second home market; and helped place hundreds of articles in newspapers and magazines.

It did not take long for others to follow the DFPA's lead. Recognizing that the second home was "becoming as all-American as automobiles and TV," the Western Wood Products Association (WWPA) published its first plan book in 1960.[21] *Vacationland Homes* included eleven designs developed by a local ad hoc plan service, Vacationland Home Plans, Inc. Each home showcased a different wood species sold by WWPA members. On the cover an A-frame called the Engelmann Spruce had the same gracefully simple appearance that made the Leisure House so compelling almost ten years

OPPOSITE **DFPA illustration of the many uses of plywood in a contemporary vacation home, 1962**

11
VACATION
HOME
PLANS

IN
THE
11
WESTERN
WOODS REGION
SPECIES

Good design plus good building materials blend together to make the very finest in vacationland homes—for a weekend or an entire season...down through the years. With this in mind, the member mills of the Western Wood Products Association proudly present this book of vacationland living ideas, and dedicate it to modern Americans everywhere who yearn to spend their leisure moments in the great outdoors.

From *Vacationland Homes*, 1960

earlier. The basic unit was a diminutive eighteen feet wide by twenty feet long. According to Robert Hunt, promotional director for the WWPA in the 1960s, the Engelmann Spruce model was designed from the beginning as a simple do-it-yourself project. Confirming the association's motive for highlighting the A-frame, Hunt stated that "its visual appeal had second home promotion possibilities for the lumber industry to sell more wood products."[22] He recalled that the marketing campaign, which continued with a

follow-up book and another A-frame design in 1965, was very successful, certain that thousands of A-frames were ultimately built using the Engelmann Spruce plan.[23]

The DFPA and WWPA were among the first to appreciate the rising tide of middle-class vacation homes and the special place A-frames would have in the trend. Beginning in the early 1960s, numerous other organizations, including the Southern Pine Association and the Western Pine Association, published their own plan books, pamphlets, and articles featuring the A-frame. At the same time, individual companies stepped beyond their trade organizations and began to ally themselves directly with the triangular vacation home. The goal was the same as the wood associations, to heighten their profile in the increasingly lucrative second home market and advance the idea that their products were indispensable to the proper construction of an A-frame vacation home.

Potlatch Forests of Lewiston, Idaho, perhaps more than any other company, embraced the A-frame. Its 1961 book *Free-Time Homes* offered twenty designs developed by the Home Building Plan Service (HBPS); five were A-frames.[24] Each Potlatch A-frame varied considerably from the next. There was a cross-gable design; one with a vertical wall and an entrance cut into one side; an elaborate I-shaped version, complete with vertical masonry walls; and two basic versions without dormers, inset walls, or additional gables. The smallest was a mere 380 square feet, while the largest provided more than fifteen hundred square feet of living space. With this range of designs, Potlatch appealed to those looking for a step up from the shack, as well as customers interested in a vacation house with year-round house dimensions and amenities.

Free-Time Homes was revised and expanded a year later, indicating the success Potlatch

Cover of *Free-Time Homes*, 1962

DESIGN NO. 426-1

WIDTH 22'-8"
DEPTH 36'-0"
815 SQUARE FEET
UPPER LEVEL—319 SQUARE FEET

MOST POPULAR A-FRAME IN U.S.A.

A cut-a-way drawing has been made to better illustrate the excellent manner in which this free-time home can be furnished and used for maximum comfort and enjoyment.

This truly magnificent leisure-time home is designed to easily accommodate six people by means of the six beds in three bedrooms, a generous sized dining space, ample bathroom and kitchen facilities, and a most functional arrangement of living room furnishings. Cabin may be constructed in all climates and is capable of withstanding normal snow loads. Foundation may be adjusted to compensate for uneven topography. Important information regarding methods of construction and choice of materials is covered in the working plans.

This clever A-frame design is being featured as one of our most functional Free-Time Homes. The over-all size of the building is 22/8 in width and 36/0 in depth, making a total of 1136 square feet of living space. A second story that measures 13/4 in width includes a sleeping loft that is 13/4 x 8/8 and a 13/4 x 11/6 bedroom. Large window area in gable end of A-frame building is used to advantage in lighting balcony bedroom.

3

The "most popular A-frame in U.S.A.," *Free-Time Homes*, 1962

1. LOCK-DECK BEVEL SIDING AND ROOFING

This is Lock-Deck with a lap design, combining siding and roofing in one piece. Its strength and ingenious three-piece tongue-and-groove lamination eliminates underlayment, shakes, shingles and other roofing materials.

2. LOCK-DECK ROOFING

Use as roofing wherever strength, long spans and less labor are desired. Patented tongue-and-groove lamination provides insulation and speed of application. Both rough and surfaced in Southern Pine, Idaho White Pine, Inland Cedar, White Fir and Ponderosa Pine.

3. PLYLUMBER

Laminated, tongue-and-groove boards in wide widths for structural and finish framing. Potlatch Plylumber can be used for walls, roofing and flooring. Provides economical in-place cost.

4. PLYLUMBER HARDWOOD FLOORING

A unique, functional flooring system in a three-ply laminated board with a hardwood face. Flooring is available in Oak, Pecan and other hardwood species. One-step installation eliminates sub-flooring.

These Potlatch Products Add Beauty and Quality to your "FREE-TIME" HOME...

POTLATCH FORESTS INC.

General Offices, Lewiston, Idaho
Bradley Southern Division, Warren, Ark.

pfi

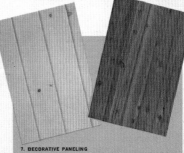

5. PLYLUMBER COMBINATION SHEATHING AND SIDING

The very latest product from Potlatch research—a lap siding lamination that completely eliminates need for sheathing . . . yet provides same protection and beauty as shingles. Outside grain is vertical.

6. LAMINATED BEAMS

Potlatch laminated beams are produced in a wide range of sizes in both Southern Pine and Northwest Soft Woods. Produced under rigid quality control to meet exacting engineering standards.

7. DECORATIVE PANELING

This finest traditional wall paneling is a specialty of both our Southern and Northwest mills. In Southern Pine or many popular patterns in Idaho White Pine, Cedar, Larch or Fir.

8. DECORATIVE PLYWOOD

Potlatch now offers new beauty in Plywood paneling. Wide choice of panels in both clear and knotty surfaced, can provide just the right touch to any room.

NOTE: Not all of these Potlatch Products are specified in every "Free-Time" home. But, all are available at local retail dealers.

Potlatch products that could be used to construct an A-frame, from *Free-Time Homes*, 1962

VACATION HOMES · RETIREMENT HOMES · BACKYARD RETREATS · RECREATION CENTERS

YOURS FOR

Care-Free Living

50¢

WITH

homasote

WEATHERPROOF
INSULATING
TERMITE PROTECTED
FACTORY FINISHED

Cover of the Homasote plan book, *Care-Free Living*, c. 1964

and the HBPS must have experienced with the first edition. The new book offered three additional A-frame designs. One was called the "most popular A-frame in the USA," another "America's leading compact A-frame." The renown these buildings supposedly enjoyed means that the HBPS had already marketed the plans before they were included in the Potlatch book. This was clearly the case with a third triangular design, which, according to the plan book, had been "given national recognition as it appeared in sixty-five major newspapers as an editorial feature and many leading magazines. Built along the McKenzie River in Oregon, this home has attracted visitors from as far away as Hawaii, California and Colorado."[25] Of course, all of the plans called for proprietary Potlatch timber products. From

Plylumber and Lock-Deck to decorative paneling, Potlatch materials would, according to the manufacturer, add "beauty and quality to the vacation home interior."[26]

Over the next decade other companies paralleled Potlatch's efforts. Georgia-Pacific, for example, distributed plans for David Hellyer's DFPA A-frame in 1960. Two years later it promoted its own design, based on the "Delta Frame, the strongest of all A-frame designs because it consists of a series of solid triangles tied to foundation piers."[27] The Homasote Company published *Care-Free Living*, with designs for twelve "easy built homes," which featured its product (a pressed board made from repulped newspapers and waterproof waxes and oils). Both the book cover and the advertisements featured A-frames. Other firms, including the Osmose Wood Preserving Company of America, the St. Regis Paper Company, Weyerhaeuser, the Simpson Timber Company, and the Masonite Corporation, also distributed plans and vacation home booklets containing A-frame designs.

A few companies relied on in-house architects to develop their vacation home plans; others contracted the design to local architects. The majority, however, relied upon "plan services," companies that normally offered plans for year-round houses but had expanded to publish plans for second homes as well. The Home Building Plan Service of Portland, Oregon, for example, developed designs for the WWPA, Potlatch, and a number of others. Chicago-based National Plan Service partnered with Homasote. These plan companies and others like them—Master Plan Service, Hudson, Garlinghouse—also published their own vacation home books. Regardless of where the designs came from, the process was the same.

Customers selected a plan, ordered a complete set by mail, and either contracted with a local builder to complete the house according to the specifications or, in some cases, built it themselves. The frequency with which A-frames appeared in these publications and the number of books that featured A-frames on the cover and in advertisements indicated the design's expanding appeal and marketability.

Perhaps the most prolific vacation home plan publisher was Home Planners, Incorporated, originally based in Detroit. The firm released editions that grew in size—*130 Vacation Homes, 151 Vacation Homes*, and *223 Vacation Homes and Plans*—throughout the 1960s. Interspersed among the log cabins, chalets, modern boxes, and octagonal designs, A-frames made up approximately ten percent of the plans offered. They ranged from humble, unadulterated triangles to larger homes with flat-roofed wings sprouting from the sides, some with dormers, others with cross gables. The designs became even more substantial over time, suggesting shifts afoot in a maturing vacation home market.

Newspapers and magazines distributed plans and advertised the publication of new plan books. It was a time when the publishing industry was experiencing its own boom; new magazines were appearing by the hundreds, and subscription bases were swelling. With postwar consumption in full swing, magazines offered the family man, seductive ski bunny, swinging bachelor, and modern housewife guidance for how to live the leisure lifestyle and what to buy to play the part. Trade associations and building companies established close relationships with these magazines, organizing partnerships in which new designs were sponsored and promotional departments were fed

stories. The DFPA, for example, mailed out a package called "Vacation Cabin Ideas for Editors" offering three complete articles, including illustrations for "real estate pages, do-it-yourself sections, building pages, Sunday supplements and home and garden sections."[28]

Popular Mechanics, working with a plan service or trade organization, ran annual roundups of new vacation home designs in which A-frames were often prominent. Similarly, both *Sunset* and *House Beautiful* published special editions devoted exclusively to vacation home designs. *Better Homes and Gardens, House & Home, American Home, Living for Young Homemakers, Field & Stream*, and *Woman's Day* regularly included one-off articles on A-frames and other vacation homes.

Articles and plan books had the shared goal of getting consumers to move from thinking about it to doing it, to buying the lumber and land and building their own piece of the good life. These publications were filled with enticing illustrations of poles doubled over with the weight of fish, endless hours of skiing, weenie roasts, and, if one desired, solitude. Always at the center was a dynamic vacation home. A-frames helped potential customers to see themselves as such, to consider a second home not as a distant fantasy but as an attainable reality.

A-frame Apogee (1962–1972)

FOR ABOUT $2000 YOU CAN WHIP UP A
SMALL, BEGUILING SHACK FROM A JACK-
STRAW-HEAP OF LOGS, BOARDS OR PLY-
WOOD SHEETS DELIVERED ON YOUR
SOME-DAY DOORSTEP—OR AS NEAR IT
AS A TRUCK CAN GO. —*LIFE* MAGAZINE, 1963

During the 1960s, the A-frame became the quintessential vacation home. It went from odd to obvious, from unusual to a ubiquitous feature of resort and recreation areas. Even the United States government was building and promoting them. Much of the A-frame's allure was its blend of affordability and excitement: visual interest at the right price. The structural efficiency of the equilateral truss and the ready availability of plywood and other modern materials helped keep costs down. Additional savings in time and money could be achieved by manufacturing parts of the structure in a factory or workshop. The resulting precut or prefabricated kits appealed to vacation community developers, local lumber companies, and do-it-yourself enthusiasts.

A-FRAME KITS

Plan books and blueprint offers spurred much of the initial interest in the A-frame. But for backyard builders who needed more than a couple drawings to get started and for developers looking for economy of scale, A-frame kits provided the answer. Relocating parts of the construction process to the lumberyard or factory had already proven successful in meeting acute postwar demands for permanent housing and rapid suburban expansion. As with the new ranch houses, made of preassembled trusses and walls, A-frame packages reduced site time, lowered unit costs, and allowed for precise control over the construction process. Needing dozens or hundreds of A-frames at a time, resort community developers saw obvious advantages in factory

Paleface Lodge and Ski Center, Jay, New York, c. 1963

production. Occasionally a development company produced its own kit in improvised workshops established for the duration of the project. Local builders created informal kits to aid their own construction of vacation homes that were offered to customers as completed "turnkey" structures. If a design turned out to be particularly popular, franchises were established and the home was marketed to the regional or national public.

Individual buyers, interested in saving money and perhaps willing to undertake at least some of the construction, remained the primary consumer of A-frame kits. With numbered parts and detailed step-by-step instructions, packages offered nonprofessionals considerable assistance while allowing them to boast of (at least partially) having built their own vacation home. But putting together a kit was not always as easy as promoters claimed. Throughout the period, magazines enjoyed gently lampooning do-it-yourself builders who got in over their heads.

At the beginning of the 1960s there were already more than one hundred vacation home packages on the market.[1] Local lumber dealers,

who would set up on the edge of recreation areas, were an important source. Some produced their own kits using original designs; others served as distributors or franchisees for nationally marketed packages shipped from distant mills and factories. Either way, customers benefited from having a local contact who was familiar with applicable building regulations and conditions, who was available to help assemble the kit, and who, if desired, could prepare foundations, plumbing, and electricity, as well as complete the interior.

Large manufacturers sold kits nationwide, making up for higher shipping costs through volume. Georgia-Pacific, Potlatch, Boise Cascade, and others saw A-frame packages as the next step beyond their plan book promotions. Companies that offered plans alone could merely *suggest* that their products were the most appropriate, while those companies that packaged kits ensured that the customer used their lumber, plywood, or laminated planks.

A-frames and the vacation home market were usually considered a sideline operation. Ernest Pierson Co. of Eureka, California, U.S. Rustic Cedar Homes in Los Angeles, and Seattle-based Lindal Cedar Homes were established housing manufacturers that expanded into the vacation home market with one or more A-frame kits. Others, like Timber-Lodge in Kansas City, Holiday House in Fort Worth, and Alpine Villages in Wilmington, Vermont, dealt exclusively in vacation home designs.

PRECUT A-FRAME PACKAGES
Precut kits were collections of the lumber, hardware, doors (and in some cases every bolt and nail) needed to build a basic A-frame shell.[2] Lumber was cut to the proper dimensions, and bolt holes were predrilled. All the bits and

Images of amateur builders who took on projects that were beyond their capabilities were common during the do-it-yourself trend's heyday, *Life* magazine, 1963

The excited owner of a Leisure House kit

pieces, however, added up to little more than a large wood tent, as most precut kits left out wiring, heating and plumbing materials, interior partitions, cabinets, and glass. In addition to finishing the interior, customers were usually responsible for site preparation, constructing the foundation, and hooking up to the electric grid, a water source, and a septic system. Some buyers—depending on their skill or daring—went it alone. It was more common that local contractors were hired to complete the task.

Packaging the kit as a shell benefited buyer and seller. New owners could decide how much of the work they wanted to do themselves and what they wanted included in the final price tag. They could tailor the interior design, leaving the floor plan open or dividing it to suit their needs. Sellers were able to market the home with an eye-catchingly low initial price and then increase the sale by including supplemental elements. Like an à la carte menu, the shell could be customized with a variety of options. Merner Lumber Company in Palo Alto, California, offered its A-frame kit, the Woodlander, in three sizes. To finish the shells, customers could then pick and choose from an interior wall kit, a plumbing kit ($500), kitchen cabinets ($135), a metal fireplace

($270), an electrical package ($155), and a redwood septic tank ($85, some assembly required). Merner even sold appliances for its kits.[3]

Occasional disparities arose between what customers thought they were getting and what arrived at the building site. Dealers, less than forthright about the contents of their kits and the additional work required before the homes could be inhabited, were often the problem. An article in *Mechanix Illustrated* warned, "Make no mistake, you've got to shop for these little domiciles with the same kind of sharp and suspicious eagle eye you cast on used car dealers." The article further cautioned customers to be on their guard against the "wily promoter" who would attempt to sell prospective buyers "just a lot of lumber you think is a house."[4]

John Campbell was the first to offer a postwar A-frame kit. Precut lumber, battens, windows, doorframes, interior partitions, moldings, bolts, nails, and front, rear, and bathroom doors were all included in the Leisure House package which could be picked up at the dealer's lumberyard or shipped by rail.[5] In a move driven more by marketing than practicality, later versions contained all of the tools needed to assemble the house, such as a hammer, level, plumb bob, wrench, caulk, and caulk gun.

in just a few days you're ready to move in—

No experience needed—all tools necessary for assembly are included with the Kit.
Your LEISURE HOUSE Kit contains easy-to-follow construction diagrams.

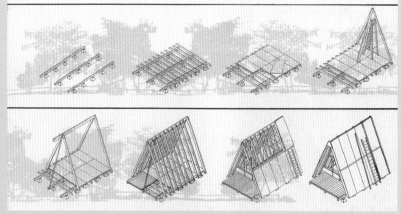

it's all yours!

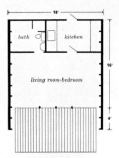

basic house

Put it where you want it—enjoy it when you want it—
and be proud of it all the time. Your LEISURE HOUSE
Kit includes everything you need to build the basic
18' x 24' unit. It is pre-cut and ready to assemble. All the
tools you will need to assemble the house are included.
No sawing is necessary. The price of the Basic House is
just $1150.00. Additional 4' Units to make the house as
large as you wish can be added for $148.00 each.

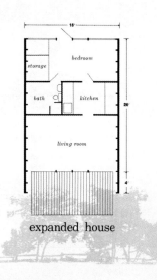

expanded house

Lindal Cedar Village of model homes, c. 1967

Others were slow to follow Campbell's lead, and throughout the 1950s the number of available A-frame kits remained low. By the early 1960s, however, timber corporations, local lumber dealers, and precut-permanent home manufacturers began developing A-frame kits. One of the largest kit manufacturers was Lindal Cedar Homes.

Sir Walter Lindal founded the company in Toronto shortly after World War II. By 1950, it was the largest North American manufacturer of precut cedar homes.[6] The company entered the A-frame vacation home market in the mid-1960s, after relocating to Tacoma, Washington. Rather than the conventional triangular truss construction, Lindal's design featured tongue-and-groove laminated planks, which functioned as structure, sheathing, insulation, and interior finish all in one. Cross members connected the two sides of the roof and functioned as joists for the loft level. Lindal's 1965 patent claimed that his design provides "a greatly simplified means and technique for erecting roof structures."[7]

The following year a *Popular Mechanics* Special 41 Page Vacation Home Issue highlighted Lindal's Aintree model on Grand Bahama

Island. Photos documented the thirty-eight-hour construction process, providing an interesting look at how the kit was pieced together.[8] Lindal later recalled receiving more than ten thousand inquiries and requests for plan books. Ads placed in *Sunset*, *Saturday Evening Post*, and other magazines throughout the second half of the 1960s further cemented Lindal's position as a leading A-frame manufacturer.[9] At decade's end Lindal Cedar Homes offered ten different A-frame kits through a network of two hundred local dealers. By 1982, when Lindal discontinued his last A-frame model, the company had sold more than seven thousand A-frame packages in North America, as well as in Japan, Korea, England, France, and Germany.[10] Lindal later credited the triangular vacation homes with spurring the growth of the company, which is now approaching its sixtieth year in business.

In the second edition of its *Free-Time Homes* plan book, Potlatch Forests included a precut "ready-to-build" A-frame package, enticingly labeled "No. PFI-40." They were joined by Serendipity Homes, Nor-West, Timberlodge, and several other companies in selling A-frame kits nationwide. Designs and structural systems varied, but the kits shared more similarities than differences. They appealed to individual buyers and developers, as well as to lumberyards and local companies that served as intermediaries between large manufacturers and their customers. Vacation home packages were often a vehicle for increasing building materials sales. They provided an affordable means for middle-class Americans to buy into postwar leisure culture. The savings of a kit compared with a custom A-frame bridged the gap between many Americans' budget and aspirations. Likewise, precut wood and precise assembly instructions filled in where the skills of the do-it-yourselfer came short.

Sir Walter Lindal, c. 1960

21 FOOT "A" FRAMES

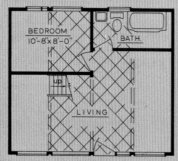

thatched area indicates second floor

ADRIAN
21'4 x 18'0

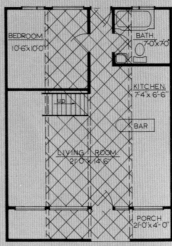

thatched area indicates second floor

AINTREE
21'4 x 29'0

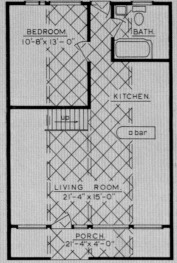

thatched area indicates second floor

APRIL
21'4 x 32'0

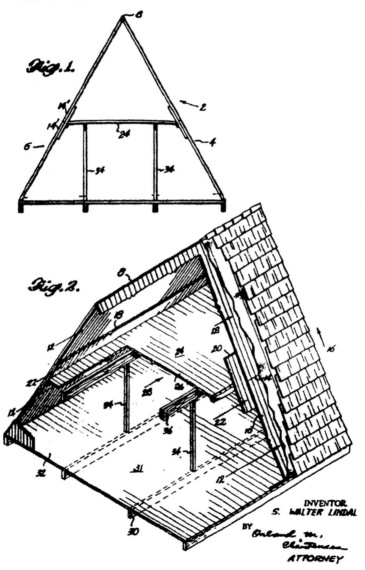

OPPOSITE **Floor plans in the first Lindal plan book to feature the patented A-frame kit, c. 1965;** ABOVE **Lindal patent, showing use of precut tongue-and-groove laminated boards as structural members**

Prefabricating A-frame gable walls in an old barn, Alpine Villages, c. 1960

PREFABRICATED A-FRAME PACKAGES

For those seeking better odds that their completed home would resemble the one shown in the brochure, prefabricated A-frames left even less work to new owners.[11] Rather than as shells, prefab A-frames were usually marketed as turnkey homes, complete in every detail. Because they could be erected quickly, these kits also appealed to real estate entrepreneurs, who needed large numbers of homes built fast. Occasionally prefabricators sold kits directly to amateur builders as "finish-it-yourself" projects, but more often prefab A-frames were marketed through local dealers, who then used their trained crews to assemble the packages.

With its uniform components, an unassembled prefabricated kit appeared much less complicated than the pile of pieces in a precut package. Most prefab A-frames were built using a series of structural sandwich panels, locked together to form roofs, floors, and gable walls. The panels were two-by-four-inch boards that formed a rectangular framework, covered on the inner and outer faces with plywood sheets. They incorporated several materials: ceiling surface, structural system, insulation, exterior sheathing, and roof shingles.[12] Panels were usually four feet wide and eight, sixteen, or twenty-four feet long, to match the standard plywood module. After assembling the panels, premade gable walls and interior partitions were then installed. By some estimates the process reduced on-site labor by eighty percent.[13]

OPPOSITE **Aintree interiors**

110

ALPINE VILLAGES, INCORPORATED

Bart M. Jacob started out as a logger who was looking for new uses for his cutover land near Mt. Snow, Vermont.[14] Within five years he had patented a prefabricated A-frame, established a company with two franchises to sell it, and made the pages of *Time* magazine. Jacob's experience illustrates how the A-frame's popularity attracted entrepreneurs who then developed and promoted designs that furthered the spread of triangular vacation homes.

Sometime in the 1950s Jacob saw photographs of a custom-designed A-frame built somewhere out west. The concept piqued his interest and, in 1958, prompted him to build twenty rental A-frames on his property, a development he called Alpstetten. Jacob prefabricated parts of the modest A-frames, making panels on jigs that were set up in an old church in Wilmington, Vermont.[15] Interest in his design grew to the point that Jacob decided to switch from being a developer to being a manufacturer, selling off all the Alpstetten cottages to concentrate on A-frame prefabrication.

In the early 1960s he founded Alpine Villages, Incorporated. The company offered several A-frame designs, each embellished to represent a different style, "from colonial American to Swedish modern to California functionalism." The majority, though, were meant to evoke Swiss mountain architecture.[16] Years later Jacob recalled that his loose application of Swiss chalet motifs, on the eaves and upper level "yodeling porch," had more to do with fulfilling skiers' expectations of what a mountain cottage should look like than with any concern for accurately recreating Swiss building traditions.[17]

Time magazine wrote about the Alpine Village A-frames in December 1961. Within weeks Jacob received more than three thousand

Alpine Villages, A-frames with what Bart Jacob called "yodeling porches," c. 1962

inquiries. The response emboldened him to develop new triangular designs that took even greater advantage of prefabrication techniques. The following summer he patented a system of interlocking component panels, which were bolted together to form the A-frame roof and walls. Jacob claimed that his attorneys spent months researching the history of prefabrication to ensure that his product was the first of its kind.[18]

In his patent Jacob stated that "the primary objective of this invention is to provide an A-frame building formed of a plurality of like modules which can be erected at the site in a matter of hours using only a few workers."[19] Structural sandwich panels extended the full twenty-four-foot height from foundation to peak.

Each side of the four-inch-thick panel had a wood flange that, when joined during assembly to the flange of an adjacent panel, appeared as a single exposed ceiling rafter. It was a crafty solution to one of prefabrication's biggest design challenges: hiding the joints between components.[20]

During the summer of 1962, Jacob formed a partnership with the panel department of Koppers Plastics Company, in Pittsburgh, to manufacture his "triangular cocoon." Koppers filled the cavity between the plywood skins with their expandable polystyrene, called Dylite. The result was a vacation home that Alpine Villages claimed was "insulated better than your refrigerator."[21] Showing the extent to which the expanding recreation and outdoor-excursion market offered new opportunities for sales and profit, Koppers's plastic insulation was also used for coolers, life jackets, and water toys. Later that year Alpine Villages signed a franchise agreement with a group of builders from Buffalo, New York, and Standish, Michigan. Called Alpine International, both operations sold packages primarily to developers and other entrepreneurs that were establishing resort communities. In exchange, the franchises paid royalties to Jacob.[22]

The company offered a variety of A-frame models—the Alpan Deluxe, the Sun-View, and the Triple A—as well as two that had vertical walls below large, steeply pitched roofs. The homes were assembled on-site by a crew of six workers, whose labor was included in the cost of the package. A promotional brochure stated that "once foundation or footings are prepared, an Alpan Chalet can be assembled and ready for interior finishing in less than two days. From the moment of decision, an Alpan Chalet can be enjoyed in less than 30 days."[23] Such speed was important, as many builders discovered that,

with the proper persuasion, vacation homes could be made an impulse buy. The promise of rapid delivery was essential to rapid turnover.

For all its innovation and hectic growth, Alpine Villages did not last long. In the wake of disagreements with a financial partner, Jacob sold his share of the company in 1963. A year later it went out of business. In all, Jacob estimates that Alpine Villages constructed more than two hundred A-frames, furthering the triangular vacation home's expansion from East to Midwest and helping to make the A-frame synonymous with New England ski architecture.[24]

Jacob's sandwich-paneled A-frame may have been the first patented version, but there were many others.[25] In Seattle Sandpoint Builder's Supply offered a modest kit, which shared many characteristics with Jacob's design but was directed toward amateur builders.[26] Aiming at a higher-end market, Leisure Homes, in Youngstown, Ohio, prefabricated turnkey A-frame models for large-scale resort developers in Ohio, Pennsylvania, and upstate New York.[27] Sensing an opportunity to

From an Alpine Villages sales brochure, 1963

Alpine Villages, cross-gable A-frame

All A-Frames are NOT alike

This one (pictured above) is ours and we are proud of it. It has an all glass gable end, 3 different living levels, 4 bedrooms, 2 baths and a large sleeping loft for weekend guests. But that's only part of our story, like our Motels, Ski Lodges and other distinctive Vacation Homes, it is built with the most maintenance free materials available and can be erected quickly and easily. Its low cost of ownership and our bank financing plan make it an outstanding value for any ski area.

Write or call for additional information on our Motels, Ski Lodges, and Vacation Homes.

STANMAR, Inc.

Boston Post Road • Sudbury, Massachusetts
TWinbrook 3-8110 • HIlltop 3-8897
FOR MORE INFORMATION CIRCLE 116 ON PAGE 27

Advertisement for Stanmar vacation homes, 1962

expand their already substantial stake in the vacation home market, aluminum and plastic companies like Kaiser Aluminum, Reynolds Metal Company, and Monsanto joined the ranks of prefabricated kit manufacturers. Just as the Koppers Company built A-frames with the same material used to keep beer cold at the beach, these companies found that the ascendant leisure culture often translated into new product lines and greater profits. Reynolds's first A-frame was a basic kit aimed at do-it-yourself enthusiasts.[28] When research suggested that more substantial versions would be more profitable, however, the company developed a new design that emphasized quality and durability, one that virtually required assembly by a contractor. Distinguishing its package from those built by amateurs, Reynolds stated that "this is not just a shack in the woods but a complete home of superior design and permanent construction, so it should be erected by a professional."[29]

Reynolds's aluminum A-frame was sold through authorized dealers as a complete home, ready for occupancy. The price included bathroom and kitchen equipment, electric wiring, hot-water heater, an electric heating system, and the cost of assembling the kit on the owner's site. Its biggest clients, however, were developers building places like Colington Harbor, on North Carolina's Outer Banks, and Holiday Village, on the Chickahominy River in Virginia, resort communities that were becoming an increasingly attractive vacation option toward the end of the 1960s.[30]

While the Reynolds package was clearly prefabricated and the Potlatch package was exclusively precut, some kits combined both techniques. For example, packages by the lumber dealer Stanmar (based in Sudbury, Massachusetts) had precut frame and joist timbers, combined with wall panels that were "componentized." Buyers could purchase either the shell or a completed home that included all labor costs.[31] Stanmar was one of the largest vacation home manufacturers on the East Coast, selling its A-frames to real estate developers and individuals through a thick network of representatives. Its focus was on New England's burgeoning ski areas.

DOWNHILL SKIING AND A-FRAMES

Customers who visited Stanmar's sales office were often shopping for their own private ski lodge. Between 1961 and 1966, the number of new downhill ski areas in the United States grew by more than fifteen percent each year.[32] Resorts popped up not just in Vermont, Colorado, and California, but on the biggest hills in Illinois, Wisconsin, and Ohio. The A-frame's popularity paralleled and fed off this phenomenal growth in part because it was driven by many of the same factors: increased discretionary income and vacation time, a cultural and political emphasis on physical vigor and outdoor recreation, greater accessibility by new roads, and more widely spread car ownership.[33]

In fact, the link between triangular structures and downhill skiing predated the vacation home boom. In the late 1930s, at Paradise Valley, Dr. David Hellyer's company built an A-frame hut to shelter the machinery for the first rope tow on Mount Rainier.[34] Hellyer's design was well suited to such a function; the lower portion of the triangle accommodated the engine, while the rope passed through a small square opening near the peak. At the time, the ski lift operated only on the weekends; because of the steep roof, a week's worth of snow did not need to be cleared away from the structure in order to get the machinery started on Saturday morning. The entire building was jacked up on posts to the average snowfall height, rather than being set directly on the ground, where it would have been half-buried by January.

Skiing got a big boost in 1960, when Squaw Valley hosted the Eighth Winter Olympic Games. The forty-seven thousand spectators who witnessed the Games in person were joined by millions who were for the first time able to watch an Olympic event on television.[35] Over

A-frame tow hut at Paradise, Mount Rainier, Washington, 2003, originally constructed in 1937

Broadmoor Ski Area, near Colorado Springs, Colorado, 1964

Courtesy, Pikes Peak Library District, photograph by Myron Wood

113

eleven days, viewers undoubtedly caught a glimpse of the pair of identical tri-gabled A-frames that were sitting prominently at the base of the slopes. Built as the Nevada Visitor's Center and the California Visitor's Center, the design featured glazed end walls, which provided sweeping views of the adjacent skating rink, ski runs, and jumping hills. Interior plans, likened to a snowflake, housed information desks, restaurants, lounges, first aid stations, rest rooms, bars, and souvenir shops.[36]

The Olympic buildings demonstrated how A-frames could offer a dramatic architectural statement while meeting the varied needs of ski-area patrons. Even before Squaw Valley,

Advertisement for Hemlock Farms in the Poconos, Pennsylvania, 1967

though, resorts were building A-frame variations for use as base lodges, restaurants, hotels, event ticket booths, and lift machinery sheds. Paleface, in the Adirondacks; Greek Peak, in Cortland, New York; Aspen Highlands, in Colorado; Taos Ski Valley, in New Mexico; Hyak, at Snoqualmie Pass, in Washington; Cascade Mountain, near Wisconsin Dells; and the Alp Horn Lodge, in Jackson, Wyoming, were just a few of the ski areas where A-frames figured prominently. Some, like the versions with overlapping gables at Aspen Highlands and Paleface, were modern designs with an air of urbane sophistication. Others played on a Bavarian or Alpine theme with gingerbread edges, carved spindles, and, in some truly incongruous cases, diamond-paned casement windows. This borrowing of European motifs, extremely common and widely popular, eventually drew the ire of critics who argued for a more contemporary, uniquely American approach to ski architecture.

Developers founded instant "villages" of vacation homes adjacent to the slopes, which were either rented for short stays or sold outright. It could be very lucrative. Large plots of land, discreetly acquired ahead of the ski trails and access roads, could later be parceled out for large profits. Some ski-area developers found

California Visitor's Center built for the 1960 Winter Olympics in Squaw Valley, 2003

Stack-gabled A-frame at Aspen Highlands ski lodge, Aspen, Colorado

that, when timed right, the process could bring in much more than lift tickets and hot chocolate served in the lodge. Hemlock Farms and Locust Lake, in the Poconos; Carrabassett Village, near Sugarloaf, in Maine; Bart Jacob's Alpstetten, at Mt. Snow; and AuSable Acres, in the Adirondacks, were some of the ski and vacation communities that offered turnkey packaged A-frames. In 1963 Stanmar provided prefabricated A-frame kits for a two-thousand-acre "showcase vacation community" at the base of Sugarloaf Mountain. Over time, the company became more involved in developing resort communities, managing and, later, owning a number of large-scale properties. [37]

BACKCOUNTRY A-FRAMES
Second home resorts attracted vacationers who wanted to get away from their daily life, but not too far away. Throughout the postwar period, a variety of outdoor recreation clubs and associations, along with state and national forest agencies, provided opportunities to get very far away. They built backcountry shelters in remote areas for short-term use by skiers, snowshoers, hikers, and hunters. Requiring designs that were easy to build and maintain, many organizations selected the A-frame. It was an obvious choice for construction sites that were far from the nearest paved road and where work was done by a small team, often composed of volunteers. Their stories were not ones of prefabrication and modern materials. Workers obtained concrete aggregate from nearby streambeds and often used timber that was cut down where the A-frames went up. They hauled supplies by foot, burro, or, in some lucky cases, off-road truck. In a way, these groups brought the A-frame back to

ABOVE **Assembling the base lodge at Greek Peak, Cortland, New York, early 1960s**
BELOW **Inside the A-frame base lodge at Greek Peak**

its roots, to a time when they were built for utility rather than as cultural signifier, as a survival necessity rather than a fashion accessory.

The Sierra Club was an early adopter of the A-frame. In 1954 the Ludlow Hut was constructed as part of a plan to develop a hiking and cross-country ski trail between Highways 40 and 50, through the Sierra Nevada Mountains. It was sponsored by the family of Bill Ludlow Jr., an avid outdoorsman who was killed in the Korean War, and built by Ludlow's fraternity brothers and a team of volunteers. Two years later a second A-frame was constructed along the same trail, one day trip north of the Ludlow Hut and one day trip south of Highway 40. Named the Bradley Hut, in memory of Josephine Crane Bradley, the wife of a past Sierra Club president, the second shelter was also built with volunteer labor. Material was brought by pack train from Squaw Valley. In 1997, after the Granite Chief Wilderness area was established by the United States Forest Service (USFS), the Bradley Hut was taken down and a similar version reconstructed about four miles away.[38]

As the suitability of the A-frame for backcountry use was demonstrated by the Sierra Club and other organizations and as it grew in popularity in the mid-1960s, the A-frame received official government approval. In the mid-1950s the National Park Service built an A-frame visitor's center at Lassen Volcanic National Park, in Mineral, California. Between 1963 and 1965, the USFS constructed at least sixteen structures at Tongass National Forest and Admiralty National Monument, on Alaska's Alexander archipelago. A team of USFS employees built them to shelter visiting garnet seekers, river runners, fishers, bear watchers, and bear, moose, and goat hunters. One of the A-frames, Shakes Slough #2, was originally constructed over a net-dyeing tub that had been converted to a makeshift spring-fed hot tub. All of the structures could be reached by boat or bush plane only.[39]

The designs had several gable-end configurations, some with considerably more glass than one would expect for such isolated buildings. Constructed on concrete piers, they featured an upper-level sleeping loft, running the length of the cabin, accessible through a wall-mounted ladder and trapdoor. The main level was outfitted with plywood sleeping platforms

Sierra Club's reconstructed Bradley Hut, 2000

on either side of the door; a plywood counter, secured to the sloping roof; a freestanding plywood table and benches; and a heating stove. No sink. No toilet.

Government interest in the form was further confirmed with the publication of two A-frame designs by the parent agency of the USFS, the United States Department of Agriculture (USDA). Though it usually offered designs for farmhouses, cattle feeding shelters, and horse sheds, the USDA's Cooperative Farm Building Plan Exchange series distributed A-frame plans in 1964 and again in 1968. The leaflets provided an overview of the design; a complete set of plans could be obtained from extension offices at state agricultural colleges. It was one way the government encouraged recreational spending and the utilization of forest and agricultural areas for leisure-time pursuits. By offering vacation home plans, the USDA also confirmed that recreation areas and leisure landscapes were encroaching on farmland that was amid desirable scenery and increasingly within reach of cities.[40]

When federal agencies turned to the A-frame for rural and wilderness structures, it was a sign that the form had fully achieved mainstream status: sanctioned by the Federal Government, the triangular vacation home had come a long way from its formative years, when those seeking a visually exciting, whimsical retreat had to cajole local design review boards and risk the reproach of their neighbors.

ABOVE **Backcountry A-frames in Tongass National Forest, Alaska, c. 2000 photographs**

OPPOSITE **USDA A-frame plan, 1968**

A·FRAME CABIN

COOPERATIVE FARM BUILDING

PLAN No 6003

(2 · SHEETS)

PLAN EXCHANGE

STORAGE — KITCHEN — BATH — STORAGE

DINING

STORAGE — LIVING ROOM — STORAGE

24'

24'

DECK

12' x 16'

The A-frame cabin, a very popular type of recreational second home throughout the United States, has been built by many people in mountain areas, at the shore from Maine to Florida, and across the country. Like the traditional cabins, this A-frame cabin provides quite comfortable living space for a family of four or five members. Sleeping space for weekend visitors can easily be provided by rearranging the furniture in the large bedroom on the second floor.

The first floor of this 24- by 24-foot cabin contains a living-dining room, a compact kitchen, a bathroom with shower, and adequate storage space. The living-dining room runs the full width of the building with storage space on each side.

The locale and climatic conditions are major factors for the builder to consider when deciding if a heating system and insulation are needed.

Washington, D.C.

Issued October 1968

UNITED STATES DEPARTMENT OF AGRICULTURE Miscellaneous Publication No. **1093**

For sale by the Superintendent of Documents, Government Printing Office
Washington, D.C. 20402 · Price 5 cents

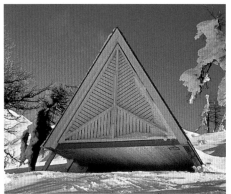

Images of Heidi and Peter Wenger's 1955 Trigon Chalet, Birg, Switzerland, after 1976 renovation

THE A-FRAME ABROAD

When *Time* magazine interviewed the Vermont prefabricator Bart Jacob, he said, "I went to Switzerland and I didn't see any A-frames; then I went to Norway and Denmark and saw lots of them. When I asked where they got the idea, they told me, 'From the U.S.'"[41] Whether the emergence of A-frames on the Continent and elsewhere was inspired by its popularity in postwar America is hard to say. A-frames from the United States appeared regularly in European design publications throughout the late 1950s and 1960s; international architects visiting recreation areas in the United States would likely have come across an A-frame or two during this period.

The triangular building had, of course, never fully disappeared from European architectural thought. Victor von Gegerfelt's stave-triangle system and Teapot Hall were built in the late nineteenth century; Artaria, May, and others resuscitated the idea in the early 1900s. Even before Campbell and Wong's Leisure House made its debut at the 1958 Brussels exposition, postwar designers outside the United States were building triangular homes for recreation and relaxation. Perhaps the most publicized European postwar A-frame was the Trigon Chalet designed by the Swiss architects Heidi and Peter Wenger.[42]

On an Alpine mountainside over six thousand feet above the Rhône Valley and a half hour's walk from the nearest road, the house provided a secluded retreat from the Wengers' office in Brig, Switzerland. Just out of school at the time, the Wengers' design was a fairly conventional A-frame. Setting it apart, however, was the way the Trigon was closed up when unoccupied. Like a triangular drawbridge, a wood-plank shutter could be raised to shield the gable-end windows. When lowered by rope and pulley, the shutter formed a deck that cantilevered over the mountainside.

In the late 1960s the Wengers' trips to the cabin became less frequent. No longer satisfied with the design, they set about refashioning it. Completed in 1976, the new version replaced the rectangular windows with a triangular sash that pivoted open, allowing ventilation and access to the deck. A barrel-shaped basement was added below the triangle, along with a spiral staircase that connected all the levels.

Trigon interior

Smaller triangle shutters were added to the secondary gable end. Most dramatic, the Wengers cleared out the interior partitions, making a unified open space, more fully integrating the inside of the house with its stunning location. The interior was complemented by furniture the couple custom-designed (including a table set in the floor and a spherical sink and cabinet unit) "according to the inner form" of the house, "so that it should not look like an attic."[43]

Two years after the Trigon was built, architect Folke Hederus built an A-frame summer home in Swedish Lapland more than one hundred miles north of the Arctic Circle. Named

for its owner, the director of a nearby iron mine, Martin's Stuga was a simple wood design with a single dormer opening up the main living area. The gable ends had square windows set between clapboard siding. Like so many American versions, the kitchen was to the rear of the open living area, beneath a two-bunk loft.[44] A year after Hederus built Martin's Stuga, another architect from Sweden, Svend Bøgh-Andersen, offered plans for another modest A-frame in a Swedish home magazine. Reflecting the rustic approach to vacation home design common in Scandinavia, Bøgh-Andersen's scheme did not include a bathroom within the

Trigon interiors

main structure. Instead, the architect provided an adjacent A-frame outhouse, about half the height of the main A-frame connected with a narrow deck and trellis.[45]

Throughout the 1960s, the A-frame vacation home continued to spread throughout Europe. Custom designs by Per Cappelen in Norway, Jacob Blegvad in Denmark, and Julio Garcia Lafuente in Italy introduced new variations and interpretations. As in the United States, there were amateur built A-frames, as well as precut and prefabricated kits. They appear to have been a particularly popular form of recreation structure in Poland, Czechoslovakia, and other countries in the former Eastern Bloc, where they functioned as state-sanctioned mountaineering cabins and resorts operated by unions, employee organizations, and clubs. Somewhat more exclusive was a hunter's lodge designed by Soviet architect Igor Vasilevsky, built outside Moscow in 1964. Made with pine logs and filled with custom furniture, the lodge was part of a recreation complex reserved for the exclusive use of high-level Communist Party members.[46]

A-frames also made inroads beyond continental Europe. A collection of triangular cabins built in the late 1960s as a "municipal rest camp" in Swakopmund, near Namibia's famed sand dunes, and a group that originally served as staff housing at a resort on Rarotonga, in the Cook Islands, are just a few examples. In Japan architect Masako Hayashi developed two elegant interpretations in the mid-1960s: a club on the Izu peninsula and a private country home in the resort areas of Naka-Karuizawa.[47] Both were built for families eager for the occasional escape from their Tokyo apartments. They shared many features with American A-frames—glass gable ends, vertical walls set within the angled roof rafters, and interior lofts—but the treatment of these elements was heavily influenced by Japanese building traditions. Round pole rafters and purlins, for example, replaced dimensioned lumber, and rounded timbers were set against diagonal plank sheathing to resemble the underside of a thatched roof. A design for another A-frame in Karuizawa displayed a similar convergence of contemporary triangular design and vernacular motifs.[48] Developed by the Nikken Architectural Office, the mountain lodge had rounded beams, diagonal sheathing, and large sliding glass doors, which opened onto a front deck below a loft porch.

After World War II, as in ancient times, the A-frame transcended climate and culture. Whether prefabricated ski chalets in Vermont or meticulously crafted houses on the Japanese coast, triangular structures represented escape and holiday living. But, as in ancient times, the A-frame also resisted a narrow definition of its function. During the 1950s and 1960s, the A-frame's flexibility was demonstrated by variations designed for commerce and worship that appealed to the lowest common denominator as well as the highest human aspirations.

Martin's Stuga, designed by Folke Hederus, near Kirune, Sweden, 1957

Beyond the Vacation Home

ISN'T ALL THIS EXACTLY WHAT THE CHURCH
BUILDER HAS BEEN LOOKING FOR ALL THE AGES
PAST—GREATER SPAN, HEIGHT, LIGHTNESS,
OPENNESS, ACOUSTICAL CONTROL, EASE OF
CONSTRUCTION, SIMPLE METHODS?
—ARCHITECT PAUL THIRY, 1955

A short time after A-frame vacation homes hit the pages of *Architectural Record* and *Arts and Architecture*, the triangular form made its way into ecclesiastical and commercial architecture. A-frame churches became a common sight as new communities sprang up in the suburbs and existing congregations modernized to accommodate an expanding postwar population. That a building type increasingly used for play was effortlessly being adapted as a place to pray seems to have caused little concern—in the United States or abroad. In new resort areas and suburban shopping strips A-frame motels, restaurants, liquor stores, and pet shops fought for the attention of consumers. They often got it, with the help of bright paint jobs and neon signs. By the 1960s, the A-frame was considered appropriate not only for relaxation and recreation but also as a sacred space and place of business.

THE SYNTHESIS OF SIGNAGE AND
STRUCTURE

The joining of A-frames and commercial activity was natural. Even at the peak of their popularity in the mid-1960s, triangular buildings were still odd enough to attract attention. A-frame flower shops and motorcycle dealers stuck in the minds of potential customers. No one used a colonial-revival barbershop to give directions, but "Turn left at the A-frame" or "It's the A-frame on the corner" was exactly the kind of recognition owners sought. Businesses often made the most of the prominent roof by painting it bright colors or covering it with stripes. Several A-frame business owners likened the large pitched roof to a billboard. At a time when design restrictions and sign ordinances were rare, an A-frame could be the boldest building on the block.

Liquor store built from a Lindal Cedar Homes kit, c. 1968

LEFT **A-frame motorcycle shop on Route 1S in 2003, Massachusetts**
RIGHT **A-frame liquor store in 1999, Big Bear, California**

A-frame businesses often appeared around ski areas. In addition to the triangular lodges and lift ticket booths within resorts, A-frame motels, restaurants, and city welcome centers could be found in the towns and on the roadsides nearby. Eventually A-frame businesses turned up in areas not known for outdoor recreation opportunities, and the services they offered and the products they sold were totally unrelated to skiing, boating, or "getting away from it all."

Perhaps the most common triangular commercial function was the A-frame motel. There were two general models: the first was based on the prewar "cottage court," or "tourist court" with individual cabins; the second was motor lodges that incorporated triangular design elements.[1] Cottage court A-frames were either set close to one another in a clearing beside the road—where their shapes could be

Ranch Motel logo

noticed by passing cars—or spaced further apart in the woods connected by foot paths to a main lodge. The latter was a similar arrangement to that of postwar vacation communities, except that the cottage court A-frames were usually more modest and were rented by the day or week, rather than individually owned.

Entrepreneurs who set up cottage court A-frame motels, like many other A-frame business owners, often relied on precut or prefab kits. It was an opportunity of which package designers were well aware. The earliest advertisements for John Campbell's Leisure House, in 1952, proposed it for use as a motel unit. Ten years later the Merner Lumber Company, in Palo Alto, California, described its El Ranchito model as "eminently suitable for use as a motel unit. Proof that this market exists is the fact that six of the large El Ranchitos were sold to a motel operator before the cabin was built." Flander's Lumber Company, of Essex Junction, Vermont,

Twenty-five individual A-frame units at the Ranch Motel, Rice Hill, Oregon, 2003 photograph

sold its precut A-frames throughout the state as a detached motel.[2]

Conventional roadside motor lodges also worked A-frame forms into their designs. Many, like the Safari Inn in Murfreesboro, Tennessee, used the triangle as the motel office, with attached one- or two-story guest-room wings extended from the sides of the triangular roof. Other designs, such as the Travelers Rest Motel in Everett, Pennsylvania (1964), had room blocks that were separate structures from the A-frame office. In both cases, the A-frame formed a focal point, increasing the visibility of the low-slung buildings while indicating where arriving guests should check in.

Travelers Rest Motel dated to the 1930s and had been in Roger Bowman's family since 1947.[3] Living in California in the early sixties, Bowman had seen a lot of A-frames. When his father died and Bowman headed back East to take over the business, he brought along plans to build a new A-frame home and office. He and his wife, Karen, ordered a kit through a California company and picked it up in Pennsylvania. When constructed, the A-frame looked like any other triangular home. Only the carport attached to the front indicated the commercial function of half the building. Obviously pleased with the result, the Bowmans decided to expand the following year. Working with a local architect, they came up with a cross-gable restaurant, to be built next to the A-frame office and house. The restaurant bore an unmistakable resemblance to another triangular motel building, the Howard Johnson's cross-gable office.

Introduced in 1958, the "Gate Keeper" A-frame accompanied Howard Johnson's expansion into franchised motor lodges and was a significant departure from the restaurant chain's earlier use of Georgian motifs.[4] The building's

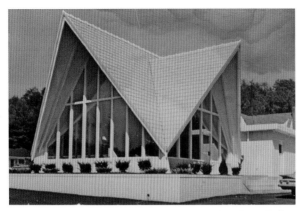

Travelers Rest restaurant, exterior and interior, Everett, Pennsylvania, c. 1965

chief appeal, of course, was its large porcelain enamel roof, an abstract orange sign that could easily be seen in time for speeding cars to opt for the off-ramp. The roof was made of two intersecting gables, the lower edges of which joined at concrete buttressed points just above ground level. Both gables had glass window walls beneath their swept-back profiles, and the upper ridgeline was topped with an elongated green weathervane. Part carryover from the New England-farm motif of the old restaurant, part space-age antenna, the spiked weathervane presented a seemingly contradictory

 *(Howard Johnson image)*

Howard Johnson's Motor Lodge with cross-gable A-frame office, c. 1960

Lake County (IL) Discovery Museum/Curt Teich Postcard Archives

OPPOSITE **Travelers Rest menu**

image. Adeptly blended into an A-frame form, however, Howard Johnson had it both ways: it was exciting, contemporary, and attention getting, with elements of the familiar and even the traditional.

Howard Johnson represented perhaps the only case of a major motel chain's using the triangular form. Most A-frame motels were one-offs, individually owned enterprises like the Travelers Rest. A-frame fast food restaurants were also primarily mom-and-pop operations, with two prominent exceptions. Beginning in the early 1960s, both the Whataburger hamburger chain and the Der Wienerschnitzel hot dog franchise relied on triangular buildings to attract customers and serve as symbols for their business.

In 1961 the Corpus Christi–based Whataburger Company adopted an orange-and-white striped A-frame as the new model for its expanding chain of hamburger stands.[5] Over thirty feet tall and abundantly lit, the structure was easily seen and remembered. It was featured on drink cups and burger wrappers, on uniforms,

Whataburger at night

and in advertisements. The Whataburger A-frame was logo, sign, and structure, all rolled into one, a quintessential example of what cultural geographer John Jakle has called "place-product-packaging."[6]

Whataburger was founded in 1950 by Harmon Dobson, an Arkansas-born oil engineer, car salesman, and diamond merchant. His first stand, selling quarter-pound hamburgers for thirty-five cents, was a twelve-by-sixteen-foot prefabricated steel box. Similar structures with just a walk-up window and kitchen were used when Dobson opened additional locations and began to franchise. The main box was set against a long canopy, which protected cars from the Texas sun and increased the stand's profile. Designs did vary, however, as Dobson strove for greater efficiency through different kitchen and serving configurations and sought the best ways to lure customers.

By the late 1950s, there were more than twenty Whataburgers scattered across Texas. One version, in McAllen, Texas, featured a striped sign rising straight up from the canopy. Atop the panel was the company's name, written in large letters, a bold effort to increase the visibility of what was otherwise a horizontally

oriented building. Though not widely adopted, the striped sign was the clear precursor of Dobson's next experiment.[7]

For unit twenty-four in his expanding hamburger empire, Dobson decided to abandon a box design that was getting lost along the increasingly cluttered and cacophonous roadside. He upped the ante with a triangular form that was higher and brighter than anything else on the commercial strip. A young Corpus Christi architect named John M. Olson turned Dobson's "back-of-the-napkin sketch" into buildable plans. Tom Moore, a steel fabricator who had built Dobson's earliest walk-up stands, was brought back to oversee construction of the new A-frames.

The first Whataburger A-frame opened in March 1961 in Odessa, Texas. Five steel I-beam trusses, connected by steel purlins and crossties formed the basic structural shape. Orange and white corrugated-steel panels covered the roof and the gable ends, while an aluminum framework around the entrance supported painted fiberglass panels and windows. A diamond-shaped canopy extended from the building entrance, providing shelter for cars and customers seated at outdoor tables. The air-conditioned interior was a tight fit for the kitchen, serving counter, and the small space where lines would form. No indoor seating was provided. Large signs on both the A-frame peak and canopy read simply *Whataburger*.

In a 1964 brochure directed at potential Whataburger franchises, Dobson explained why he chose the A-frame design:

> It has been our experience that a distinctive building you can't help but see, with lighting and signs you can't help but notice, plays an important part in gross sales. We could almost be

133

OPPOSITE TOP **First Whataburger A-frame, in Odessa, Texas, c. 1961;** OPPOSITE BOTTOM LEFT **Whataburger under construction;** OPPOSITE BOTTOM RIGHT **Whataburger unit in Weslaco, Texas, with upper deck seating**

accused of overdoing these features, but we know that it sells merchandise. There are more than 6,500 watts of fluorescent and quartz-iodide lighting, plus over 80 feet of turquoise neon. The orange and white metal panels on both building and canopy have become a Whataburger trademark, and Whataburger can be recognized as far as can be seen. The giant ridge row sign on top of the building can be read at a distance of more than a mile[8]

The A-frame remained Whataburger's exclusive building form throughout the 1960s. Later variations included a second-floor outdoor dining space, located within the recessed area beneath the gable; the addition of angled I-beams to form a *W* on the upper portion of the A-shape; and, in some cases, the enclosing of the gable end. A few designs had roof panels extending to the ground along the entire length of the roof; others featured inset windows along the sides. Several of the early box stands were remodeled with the addition of an A-frame to the rear of the original building. In time, the first A-frames were also revisited with enclosed dining rooms, replacing the parking canopy.

More than eighty A-frame Whataburgers were built throughout Texas, Arizona, and Oklahoma before the company introduced a "modern A-frame" (with a hipped roof) in 1974. The departure from the triangular form was in response to the increasing presence of municipal design guidelines and zoning restrictions, meant to discourage the type of building that had been instrumental to Whataburger's rise. The need for larger indoor seating areas, the cost of structural steel, and the hassle and expense of maintaining the expansive roof were

also factors. With so much of the company's history and image wrapped up in the A-frame, however, Whataburger continued to incorporate the triangular motif into several of its later designs, including the Corpus Christi flagship unit built in 1999.

Less than two years after Dobson's first triangular Whataburger was built, the California hot dog chain Der Wienerschnitzel also turned to a triangular design. Like Whataburger, the Wienerschnitzel A-frame replaced a smaller, less conspicuous box-shaped building. With a red aluminum-shingled roof, the first Wienerschnitzel A-frame was built on the Pacific Coast Highway in Long Beach, California, in 1962.[9]

In time, Wienerschnitzel added a drive-through that passed right through the middle of the building. This unusual configuration helped customers unfamiliar with the relatively new trend in fast food find the place to pull up and order. Wienerschnitzel's motive for selecting the A-frame was the same as that of other businesses. Company founder John Galardi remarked that the triangle shape "doubled the exposure of the building. It looked like a billboard lowered onto the street."[10] Of the 334 Wienerschnitzel locations in business in 2003, 145 were A-frames.

Whataburger, Wienerschnitzel, Howard Johnson, and other A-frame chains used the structure as an instantly recognizable symbol of their businesses. Like White Castles and the distinctive Golden Arches that flanked early McDonald's buildings, the A-frames were sign as architecture. They were a phenomenon that architects Robert Venturi, Denise Scott Brown, and Steven Izenour would recognize and celebrate in Las Vegas a decade later.[11] These businesses, along with the thousands of individual

One of the original Wienerschnitzel A-frames, built in the early 1960s, before the drive-thru

entrepreneurs that adopted A-frames, counted on the curiosity aroused by the quirky triangular shape, or at least on its brute visual force, to attract customers and increase sales.

A-FRAMES POINTING TO HEAVEN
The 1950s saw an unprecedented boom in religious-building construction, driven by a growing churchgoing population, which was expanding out to new suburbs.[12] Freed from wartime building restrictions and catching up with a lag

in construction that dated back to the Great Depression, it was estimated that ninety percent of the congregations in the United States were involved in some type of building program. As many as half of the new churches had modern designs.[13]

Just as the A-frame vacation home sprang from an atmosphere of architectural experimentation, the triangular-shaped church was part of an exciting trend toward creative church design. No longer beholden to a single predominant style, ecclesiastical architecture featured an expansive vocabulary of materials and almost limitless variety of forms after the war.[14] *Contemporary* was a term applied to Mies van der Rohe's stark brick-and-glass cubical chapel at the Illinois Institute of Technology; Felix Candela and Pier Luigi Nervi's concrete churches, which were at once sculptures and engineering feats; and a great number of imaginative designs in between. Architects such as Pietro Belluschi, Barry Byrne, Eero Saarinen, and Marcel Breuer developed innovative forms, expressive of the individual congregation's beliefs, responsive to its priorities, and appropriate to its budget. The goal was a "sense of spiritual immediacy."[15] Designs often borrowed materials from industrial construction: precast concrete, glue laminated rafters, open web trusses, and plywood rigid frames.

In the architectural and popular press, contemporary churches were set against what were disparagingly referred to as "period," "archaeological," or "regurgitated" forms. On the heels of the American victory in World War II, contemporary church architecture was of triumph and optimism, appropriate to a nation that considered itself blessed by God's favor. Yet traditional designs based on historic styles retained considerable support, especially among regular churchgoers. Deep divisions developed regarding which path to follow; in some cases building committees were pitted against the congregations they were supposed to represent.

A product of these currents, with one foot in the present and one in the past, the A-frame church was among the most favored forms of postwar religious architecture. It appeared shortly after A-frame vacation homes started attracting attention in the early 1950s. By the end of the decade, triangular churches were fea-

tured frequently in architectural magazines and books. They were built of concrete, wood, and steel; small or with seating for more than six hundred; by internationally recognized architects and recent graduates; and throughout the United States and abroad.[16]

In America, A-frames built for recreation stimulated the development of A-frames built for religion. Triangular churches may also have been influenced by a design that predated the postwar vacation home boom. Constructed in 1947, Frank Lloyd Wright's Unitarian Meeting House, in Shorewood Hills, Wisconsin, was dominated by a steeply pitched copper roof, whose peak rose from the single story rear entrance to a large prow-shaped window in front.[17] Whereas later A-frame designers opted for a simple glazed gable end that emphasized its own transparency, Wright chose to make his gable end the focal point of both the interior and the exterior. Inside, vertical walls of elongated masonry were counterpoised by a bare white ceiling that receded upward to meet the gable end. It was certainly a different atmosphere than the enclosed, tunnel-like feel of some A-frames that followed.

In 1953 Wright shared his motive for using the all-roof form:

> Unitarians believed in the unity of all things. Well, I tried to build a building here that expressed that overall sense of unity. The plan you see is triangular. The roof is triangular and out of this—triangulation—(aspiration) you get this expression of reverence without recourse to the steeple. The roof itself, covering all, all in all and each in all, sets forth—says what the steeple used to say, but says it with greater reverence, I think, in both form and structure.[18]

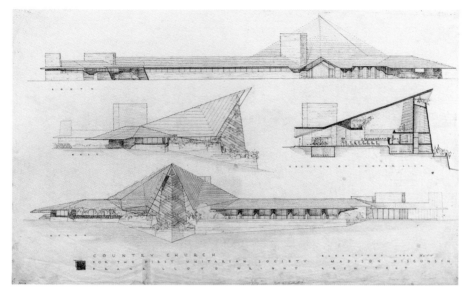

TOP **Frank Lloyd Wright's Unitarian Meeting House, elevation and section, Shorewood Hills, Wisconsin, 1947;** ABOVE **The prow-shaped gable end of the Unitarian Meeting House**

What was it about A-frames that so many church designers found appealing? Why was a form that was increasingly associated with downhill skiing and fun also appropriate for places of quiet introspection and spiritual renewal? Some explanations were pragmatic, others symbolic. No one conceded, however, that the shape was selected in part because it was popular, because even church design is subject to fashion.

Different congregations (and different congregants) held varying interpretations of what the A-frame shape meant. To many Christians, the triangular form was a three-dimensional representation of the Holy Trinity. Some found that the A-frame's stripped-down planes and straight lines reflected a modesty and purity they associated with their faith. Some saw the A-frame as a modern abstraction of the gothic cathedral, boiled down to its essential characteristics of vertical striving and soaring interior space; the peaks and spires of cathedral architecture carried through in the A-frame's emphatic roof peak and steep slope. Others held an anthropomorphic interpretation of the sloping roof. The pastor of Trinity Lutheran Church in Columbia, Missouri, stated that "the use of the A-frame structure was helpful for worshipers to be reminded of the folded hands in prayer."[19]

Postwar construction was expensive, skilled craftspeople were in short supply, and the trend was toward a greater number of congregations with fewer members. Architects seeking to create dramatic spaces with limited resources often turned to the triangular shape. As vacation home designers had found, the A-frame's structural economy provided a lot of drama for the dollar, as soaring interiors were not compromised by truss work or intrusive columns. Costs could also be kept in check by the same means used to save money on vacation home construction: modern materials and factory production. During the 1950s, at least one company made prefabricated A-frame churches. Creative Buildings, Incorporated (CBI) provided a complete church package (including stained-glass windows), designed and fabricated at its plant in Urbana, Illinois. Throughout the 1960s and into the next decade, CBI sold modified A-frame packages, although it relied increasingly on other church designs which were built with enormous glue-laminated wood arches.[20]

St. Ambrose Episcopal Church in West Fort Lauderdale, Florida, was built in the late 1950s from thirty-eight precast, prestressed concrete panels. Measuring more than thirty-eight feet long and five and a half inches thick, they had steel plates embedded in the ends and along the sides that were used to weld the panels to each other and to the foundation. On the exterior, the panels were left exposed and the joints were coated with roofing material, while an acoustical spray-on plaster was applied to the interior surface. Five openings at ground level on each side of the roof were the main sources of natural light.[21]

Advertisement for Lehigh Cement Company, featuring a concrete A-frame church, 1958

Although the triangular form made for a powerful sanctuary space, it was less successful at accommodating the many functions demanded of postwar churches. The solution was to locate meeting rooms, Sunday schools, kitchens, and offices in a cellar or in a wing extending from the sides of the A-frame. When wings were appended to both sides, the distinction between an A-frame and a conventional building with a steeply pitched roof was often lost. In some designs the roof rafters were left exposed on the interior and exterior gable ends and carried through the wings to reveal the triangular structure within.

Saints Philip and James Episcopal Church in Morenci, Arizona, was typical in its accommodation of administrative, social, and outreach functions. Constructed in 1961, the A-frame sanctuary had a knotty-blond-pine interior, matched by pine pews. The wing, looking like a ranch house with a pitched roof and clapboard siding, extended from one side of the A-frame.[22] It was a modest variation on Wright's Unitarian Meeting House, successfully combining an unassumingly dramatic worship space with a low horizontal wing devoted to church programs.

Along the south roof pitch of the Saints Philip and James A-frame, a small cross-shaped window opening was placed, which threw a symbolic light onto the wall above the altar. Triangular forms, whether high-style or humble, allowed ample opportunity for such dynamic glazing and lighting schemes. The strategic placement of skylights and light troughs and variations in gable-end window treatments could compensate for the inherently dark interior of a large A-frame structure. When applied with creativity, they could also complement the form, playing off the sloped walls and painting the interior with points of directed light. Eero Saarinen's Kramer Chapel at Concordia Senior College, in Fort Wayne, Indiana, skillfully incorporated windows to accent the triangular shape, mitigate its drawbacks, and heighten the impact of its spatial purity.

The Chapel was the centerpiece of a twenty-five-building campus, designed entirely by Saarinen's office between 1953 and 1957, for students preparing for the Lutheran ministry. Saarinen, who had just completed the General Motors Tech Center and would later design the TWA Terminal at JFK Airport in New York, the John Deere Headquarters in Moline, Illinois, and the Gateway Arch in St. Louis, brought a considerable reputation to the project.[23] Trained in the architectural office of his father, Eliel Saarinen, Eero had developed a distinctive approach to design. Though no two commissions looked alike, all of his work showed a sym-

Saints Philip and James Episcopal Church, constructed in 1961, 2002 photographs

139

pathy for human scale, a love of texture, and a preference for sculpted shapes. The Concordia Senior College founders counted on these skills when they hired Saarinen to turn a cornfield into a campus for 450 divinity students.

After his office conducted a thorough study of the future college's needs, Saarinen decided to create a number of smaller buildings—a library, a gymnasium, a chapel, classrooms, dormitories, and administrative offices—rather than placing all the functions in one or two large structures. It was an idea modeled on a northern European village. Designed last, the chapel was the centerpiece of the campus. Saarinen came up with the triangular form and then passed some sketches on to Glen Paulsen, his chief designer on the project. Paulsen then developed a number of conceptual drawings of the chapel. One proposal had vertical walls at the base and triangular windows spaced like dormers along the steeply pitched roof. An interior drawing of another proposal showed crisscrossing beams that spanned a triangular nave like traditional scissor trusses. On both the inside and outside, the final version would be a much cleaner, more austere design.

Eero Saarinen (left) and senior designer Glen Paulsen at the dedication of Concordia Senior College, 1958

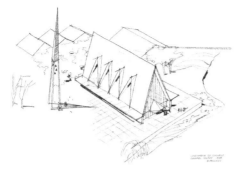

Glen Paulsen, concept sketch for the Concordia Senior College Chapel, Fort Wayne, Indiana, 1954

Set on the highest ground in front of a man-made pond, the chapel incorporated many of the material and design elements distributed across the other campus buildings. Most important was the pitched roof. At the time, Saarinen observed that "by using it on all the buildings, the group was united in one spirit. By making the pitch of the roofs on the other buildings lower than on the chapel, the lesser buildings seemed to rise up toward the most significant one."[24] It was a particularly notable feature at a time when either the flat roof or more exotic forms, like concrete shells and folded plates, prevailed over traditional roof forms. Both gable ends were enclosed with vertically oriented, diamond-shaped bricks.[25] The roof angled twenty-three degrees off vertical (the same as the tilt of the Earth on its axis) and its surface was covered with custom-made ribbed clay tiles. To preserve the pure geometric shape, Saarinen located the rest rooms, vestry, and sacristy below grade.

Complexity and subtlety were achieved in Saarinen's triangular church with a moving application of natural and artificial lighting. A vertical strip of opaque glass along one side of the roof illuminated the tabernacle and west gable wall. Skylights ran the length of the roof peak, directing a diffused beam of light downward from the center of the building, a clear intimation of divine presence.[26] Perhaps most striking was the use of glazed panels along the lower edge of the roof. Diffused by rows of upward-sloping side baffles, the unseen windows directed sunlight along the ceiling surface, lightening its visual weight and making the otherwise looming ceiling planes appear to float above their foundations. Concealed spotlights replicated the effect during evening services. Saarinen said, "We realized that light is an effective agent in creating a spiritual atmosphere. We used very low light from the side walls as well as lighting from above to get the restful, balanced quality we sought. Additional side windows dramatized the altar as a focal point."[27]

Kramer Chapel's clean lines and pure glazing program (no colored glass to speak of), as well as the simple marble-block altar, wood communion rails, and uncomfortable pews were all purposeful. According to the Reverend Robert V. Roethemeyer, a professor at the school, they are a reflection of the stern pietism characteristic of northern European Lutheranism. Saarinen's chapel was well adapted to the Missouri Synod in particular, an austere faith that embraces bodily fasting and bodily preparation.[28]

Some thought triangular churches were appropriate to Lutheranism exclusively. In his 1962 book on modern church architecture, Albert Christ-Janer called the A-frame "one of the most popular of modern church designs," with "versions too numerous to mention." He noted the success of Saarinen's chapel but cau-

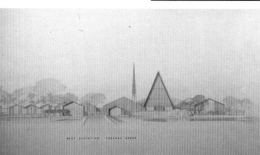

CLOCKWISE FROM TOP: **Kramer Chapel at Concordia Senior College, now Concordia Theological Seminary, main elevation, 2002 photographs; Side baffels and windows run along both sides of the nave; Looking toward the altar with the opaque ribbon window at right; Presentation drawing of the west elevation and surrounding buildings by Glen Paulsen, 1954**

tioned that "the alluring simplicity of this form and structure can lead to inappropriate uses. Denominations other than Lutheran should think twice before adopting this design so evocative of a specific cultural heritage."[29]

Of course the A-frame was never the prerogative of a single denomination. There were a large number of Lutheran A-frames, but multi-denominational A-frames were built, such as Edgar Taffel's 1966 Protestant Chapel at JFK Airport's Tri-Faith Chapel Plaza.[30] There were Roman Catholic A-frames, Episcopal A-frames, Baptist A-frames, Seventh Day Adventist A-frames, and numerous other faiths and denominations that adopted the form. The range of A-frame interpretations and adaptations seemed even greater in religious architecture than in recreational design. Some, like Saarinen's chapel, had no appurtenances to distract from their simplicity. Other designs were perhaps less chaste but still within the A-frame genre. In 1963 Skidmore, Owings and Merrill (SOM) came up with one of the most unusual variations: the Cadet Chapel at the Air Force Academy, in Colorado Springs, Colorado. Using a row of seventeen steel tetrahedron frames, SOM architect Walter A. Netsch Jr. exploded the typically flat A-frame roof plane into three dimensions.[31] It was an example of how far the triangular shape could be taken from its roots to an elaborate and thoroughly modern structural system.

INTERNATIONAL A-FRAME CHURCHES

Like the cross-pollination of A-frame vacation homes between the United States and abroad, there were numerous examples of triangular churches outside American borders. In some cases they were undoubtedly influenced by church architecture in the postwar United States. Others seem indebted to vernacular construction traditions native to their locale. Again, like the A-frame vacation home, there were triangular churches overseas that predate the widespread adoption of the form in North America.[32] They confirm that American designers were not alone in appreciating the combination of spatial solemnity and affordability inherent to the A-frame church.

Postwar religious A-frames seem to have found their widest application in Scandinavia. During a narrow period in the late 1950s and early 1960s, several were built in Norway alone. There, they were called "boathouse churches" because they resembled the triangular sheds traditionally used to shelter fishing boats in the

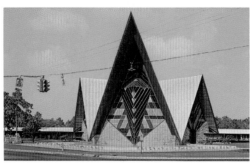

Grace Lutheran Church, St. Petersburg, Florida

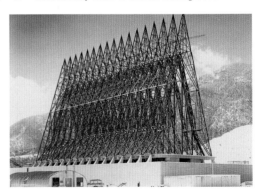

LEFT **Grace Lutheran Church, St. Petersburg, Florida, c. 1961**
RIGHT **Cadet Chapel at the Air Force Academy, Colorado Springs, Colorado, under construction, c. 1963**

LEFT **Tromsdalen Church, Tromsdalen, Norway, c. 1964;** RIGHT **Bakkehaugen Church, Oslo, Norway, c. 1959**

coastal villages. Bakkehaugen (hilltop) Church was built in Oslo, Norway, in 1959. Designed by Erling Viksjø, the structure, including the roof, choir wall, choir podium, altar, pulpit, baptismal font, and etched murals on the ceiling, was rendered completely in sandblasted concrete. Like Saarinen's Kramer Chapel, the almost monochromatic interior created a feeling of austere serenity. On the exterior, the triangular theme predominated. A sandblasted pattern of stacked triangles covered the primary gable end, while the church entrance led through a low triangular narthex.[33] A more abstract version of the A-frame church was built at Tromsdalen, Norway, touted as the northernmost city in the world. Properly known as Arctic Cathedral, Tromsdalen Church was designed by Jan Inge Hovig between 1957 and 1960 and built in 1964. It consisted of a series of triangular concrete columns, faced with lacquered aluminum plates. Like two collapsible drinking cups placed on edge, the largest triangles were located on the ends, the form narrowing progressively toward its center.[34]

Tromsdalen and Bakkehaugen churches used modern materials in different ways. Tromsdalen's successively broader profile attempted to mediate a relationship between heaven and earth, while Bakkehaugen strived to remain in the background, not interceding. In Nordseter, Norway, near the Lillehammer ski resort, another triangular church was built, whose result was quite different from that in Oslo and Tromsdalen. Constructed in 1960 for the townspeople, tourists, and visiting military crews, the Nordseter Church featured standing round timbers and appeared to be ancient rather than modern. The design emphasized the continuity of the church and an affinity with the northern landscape by evoking premodern triangular construction with a purposefully primitive application of traditional materials.

Ten years after this rush of Scandinavian A-frame construction, on the other side of the world the Unification Church in Korea selected the triangular form for its first permanent worship spaces.[35] When Reverend Sun Myung Moon founded his church in 1954, services were

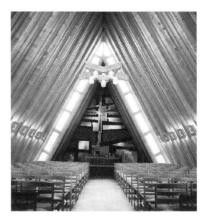

Nordseter Church, Lillehammer, Norway, c. 1960

held in rented houses and barracks. During the 1960s, as membership grew and more congregations were founded, the leaders initiated a building program. Church elder and architect Duk-moon Aum came up with the approved design. The Unification Church A-frames were wood framed, with brick gable ends and inset vertical walls in the bays behind the entrance. The interiors, sparsely decorated and without permanent seating, received plenty of daylight through casement windows located on the gable ends and inset walls. A small one- or two-room annex was placed at the back as a residence for the pastor's family. The first A-frame Unification Church was built in Shintanjin, South Korea, in 1974. In all, the Reverend Moon's followers built about 120 A-frames throughout North and South Korea.

The Unification Church structures and the A-frame chapels in Norway (where the Church is affiliated with the State) were selected by church leaders for the benefit of local congregations. In the United States, where churchgoers played a more active role in the decision

making process, the decision to build a contemporary design was often contentious. American designers and church leaders interested in constructing up-to-date forms were warned to be cautious of stepping beyond the acceptable aesthetic limits of their congregations.[36] Architecture publications offered advice about how to bring churchgoers on board, to educate and "condition" them. Alvin Rubin, the pastor of Zion Lutheran Church in Portland, Oregon—which built a Pietro Belluschi design—suggested in 1954 that many "need to be taught how to appreciate the contemporary." He encouraged pastors to "lead them into accepting the idea that they should erect a building which is an expression of their own devotion, not their fathers' or grandfathers'. This means a lot of work for you."[37]

Given the reception of A-frame church designs and the large number built throughout the postwar world, it is safe to say that they did not require the hard sell so many other designs seemed to need. Although triangular churches represented modern design in all of their salient

LEFT **Unification Church A-frame, Korea, 1989;** RIGHT **Another Unification Church, Korea, 1975**

characteristics (smooth, unadorned lines, roofs expressive of structure and the space within, use of industrial materials), they were also reassuringly familiar. A-frame churches, like A-frame vacation homes, represented a popularized modernism, palatable to a broad spectrum of worshippers.

Churches, fast food entrepreneurs, and motel proprietors turned to A-frames because they were affordable, quick to build, and impressive. The hospitality industry played on the A-frame's strong association with fashionable leisure. These businesses, along with liquor stores, coffee shops, and others, counted on the prominence of the design to attract customers. Religious congregations likewise saw advantages in the visual and spatial interest of the tri-

angular shape. It was a testament to the A-frame's broad appeal and adaptability that a form used along the roadside to sell hot dogs could, down the street, be a site of spiritual communion.

ALPAN ALPAN

The ALPAN Home, to the consumer, is an exciting, practical and high quality home designed, insulated, and made in a way to be both permanent and maintenance-free.

The ALPAN system, to the dealer and developer, is a trouble-free, efficient operation based on selling and finishing an exclusive, high-quality package that can be installed any place, any time.

The ALPAN system, to the manufacturing distributor, is a clean, profitable operation based on low overhead, simplified inventory, and protection from duplication.

The ALPAN Home—"The house costs the least to keep."

A Cultural and Marketing Icon

...TO CATCH PROSPECTS WITH ADVERTISING,
A TIME-TESTED APPROACH IS TO SHOW A
FREE-WHEELING DESIGN. A-FRAMES ARE
GOOD ATTENTION GETTERS.
—*HOUSE AND HOME MAGAZINE*, 1964

During the 1960s, the A-frame passed from object to idea. Since John Campbell's Leisure House, the triangular building had been offered up as the perfect fit for postwar attitudes toward free time and recreation. From the glazed gable walls and open plans to the easy flow from interior to spacious integrated decks, A-frames were an up-to-date alternative to traditional cabins with small windows and big fireplaces. Where others were dour, the A-frame was fun. It suggested the unabashed and active enjoyment of free time. Its elegant simplicity resonated with architectural purists. Its affordability attracted broad swaths of the middle class.

As the A-frame hit its stride, it came to be seen not only as appropriate to the new leisure lifestyle but symbolic of it. The A-frame embodied the idea of vacation, and, more broadly, the good life. It was recreation, leisure, free time, social status, physical activity, lazy indolence,

informality, escape, pleasure, success, and attainment, all distilled into a triangular form.

Recognizing this association, companies sought ways to link their products with the A-frame vacation home and the positive ideas it represented. Marketing efforts furthered the A-frame's symbolism with advertisements that used the triangular shape as an icon easily interpreted by consumers. Resort developers used A-frame models to lure customers to their new subdivisions; such models were given away in home show promotions. They were resized to infiltrate the suburban backyard and playroom, miniature versions that brought a little leisure attitude a lot closer to (the permanent) home. The most convincing indication that the A-frame had become a symbol ascribed with a significance not shared by any other vacation home design was the fact that so many companies attempted to latch onto its allure.

Alpine Villages A-frame exhibit at a home show in the early 1960s

The Swift Bermuda with beautiful curved staircase, 3 bedrooms, 2½ baths

SWIFT HOMES

You can afford a home like the beautiful new Swift Homes Bermuda.

Swift uses pre-designing, mass purchasing, precision cutting and automated manufacturing methods, along with top quality materials, to produce a fine home at big savings. You can save even more by using Swift's 11-Point Service Program to finish the house yourself.

Let Swift, one of the world's most progressive producers of manufactured homes, put you into a beautiful Swift Home of your own.

VISIT THE SWIFT DEPARTMENT STORE OF HOMES
Only one of its kind.

You'll see scale models in full color of many Swift designs, so easy to visualize. And they're shown in a full-size A-Frame store. Ask the Swift Home Consultant about

SWIFT'S
NO MONEY DOWN,
LONG TERM FINANCING
for lot owners

SWIFT HOMES, Division of Swift Industries, Inc., Elizabeth, Pa. 15037   Dept. BGH

Please send me the FREE, full-color Swift Homes catalog and the name and address of my local Swift Homes dealer.

Name_____

Address _____

City, State and Zip Code_____ Phone_____

I own a lot ☐   I can get a lot ☐

Developers, contractors and vacation home manufacturers erected model A-frames and placed them along the road or at the entrance to new resorts to attract curious potential customers. The A-frame was bait, a lure to attract customers who could then be introduced to a wider selection of vacation homes, year-round homes, or unimproved lots. Stanmar president Stanley Miller found that "many buyers consider the A-frame to be synonymous with vacation homes. They request information on A-frames but when they see other models they usually choose something entirely different."[1] In Miller's experience, the A-frame functioned like a flashy sports car in an auto showroom: it generated excitement and brought in customers, who then saw the whole line of models and ended up with something more conventional.

A-frames could also spur permanent home sales. Swift Homes, based in Elizabeth, Pennsylvania, used the A-frame to market its line of year-round ranch houses and split-levels. One of the largest postwar prefab-home manufacturers in the United States, the company dabbled in the leisure market with a single precut vacation home kit.[2] Arrangements between Swift and its network of dealers required each franchise to build three model homes on its lot. Two had to be versions of the company's permanent homes; the third had to be the A-frame. Cardboard scale models and photographs of the company's homes were displayed in the A-frame model, turning it into a showroom called the Swift Department Store of Homes.[3] In 1962 the company exhibited its A-frame showroom on the platform in New York City's Pennsylvania Station.[4] It was great publicity, both for Swift and for A-frames in general. The triangular house, evocative of sparsely populated outdoor recreation areas, set amid the squealing brakes,

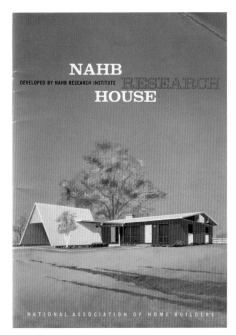

National Association of Home Builders' Research House, Fort Wayne, Indiana, 1958

shrieking whistles, and rumbling footsteps of Penn Station, must have provided an incongruous scene. Could the A-frame appeal to anyone more than to the tired commuter after a long week at the office?[5]

Partnering in the late 1950s, the National Association of Home Builders (NAHB) and the Douglas Fir Plywood Association (DFPA) used the triangular form to generate consumer interest in permanent homes. Testing modes of prefabrication, they built a "research house" in South Bend, Indiana, from structural sandwich panels. Clearly meant to spice up the otherwise humdrum design, an enormous A-frame carport, made from sixteen-foot-long panels was attached to the front of the house. It was manu-

OPPOSITE **Swift Homes' "Department Store of Homes," 1966**

LEFT **Leisure House model with recreation area landscaping, unknown exhibition, c. 1953;** RIGHT **Alpine Villages model at an exhibition, Albany, New York, c. 1963**

factured by Koppers Plastic Company, the same company that, several years later would produce components for Bart Jacob's Alpine Villages. When the model opened for visitors and their opinions were analyzed, the NAHB reported that "the unique car shelter received considerable attention with about half the people interviewed definitely not liking it and the other half saying that they were not quite sure whether they liked or disliked it."[6] It is doubtful that the NAHB was seriously proposing the A-frame carport as a suburban prototype (and if it was, the lukewarm reception probably ended such ideas); it is more than likely that they were using the triangular structure to get publicity and foot traffic to the open house.

A-FRAMES ON DISPLAY

Penn Station and the suburbs might have been unusual settings for the triangular vacation home, but the practice of exhibiting full-size models for captive audiences dates back to the first years of the A-frame boom. Since then, home shows, outdoor recreation fairs, and trade conventions regularly featured A-frame models erected by a variety of entrepreneurs and builders.[7] Local contractors, hoping to break into the vacation home market, constructed their own designs or used those offered in plan books. Kit manufacturers erected respective signature models, demonstrating how easily the parts fit together and passing out brochures and business cards. At larger shows, professional decorators were called in to complete the interiors and landscape architects worked to transform the display booth into a beach or mountain setting. Potential buyers could try out the sloped interior and sit in a butterfly chair, looking out over the other exhibits and envisioning themselves as second home owners. For some, the vacation home remained a distant fantasy; a lucky few got one sooner than they could have imagined when, on the last day, home shows raffled off the display model.

In the spring of 1960 Assembled Homes, of Winchester, Massachusetts, built and displayed David Hellyer's DFPA A-frame at the Fourth Annual New England Home Furnishings Show in Boston.[8] The house was offered as the grand prize in a drawing held on the final afternoon. The winner received the fully assembled A-frame, including draperies, carpeting, and interior furnishings "of the most modern style" provided by local businesses. (In what Dr. Hellyer must have considered a flattering error, the *Boston Herald* attributed the design to Frank Lloyd Wright.)[9] The following year the same model was built for the Home and Outdoor Living Show in Washington, D.C., where again it served as grand prize. On the last day of the show singer Jimmy Dean selected the winner's name from the "lucky barrel." Along with Hellyer's "Swiss type Vacation Chalet"—constructed by local builder Suburban Lumberteria on the winner's lot—the grand prize included a thirteen-foot "family" powerboat and three hundred dollars cash, to help buy land or furnish the new home.[10]

Libby's advertisement, 1965

MAIL-IN SWEEPSTAKES

Attending home shows and hoping for the door prize was one way to win an A-frame; mail-in sweepstakes were another. In 1962 Pittsburgh Paints and DFPA organized a promotional sweepstakes. The contest offered one hundred thousand dollars in prizes, including fishing rods, air conditioners, and Rambler convertibles. Four grand-prize winners could choose one of four DFPA vacation home models, including Hellyer's A-frame. Each home featured "log-burning fireplaces, modern baths, built-in kitchens, and spa-cious sundecks!" and would be "built on the winners' lots of sturdy weatherproof DFPA quality-tested plywood."[11] Contestants had only to go to the nearest Pittsburgh Paints dealer, fill out an entry form, get it countersigned by a salesperson, and deposit it in the contest box.

Other companies that gave away A-frames had a more tenuous connection to the building and recreation industries than a paint manufacturer. In 1965, Libby's, the canned veg-etable producer, promoted its "Cabin in the Mountains" sweepstakes with a full-page ad in

If I only had one room, the walls would be Marlite paneling.

One great room can make a whole house. And Marlite makes the room.

To begin with, Marlite is beautiful. Warm wood-grains, rich colors, decorator patterns, deep-embossed texture.

Then years go by, but the newness stays. Sealed in by a soilproof, wash-and-wear finish that scuffs and stains can't harm.

Installation? A matter of hours. In fact, the only hard part is picking one

great wall for your great room. Marlite has more than 70.

It's the Idea Paneling.

 Marlite
plastic-finished paneling

THE MARLITE WALL BOOK: 24 pages of ideas to give your home a decorator's touch. Illustrated in full color. Send coupon and 25¢ to Marlite Division of Masonite Corporation, Dept. 449, Dover, Ohio 44621.

Name
Address
City   State   Zip

Masonite advertisement, 1969

Sunset magazine. As in the Pittsburgh Paints contest, the prizes—mink stoles by Lilly Dache and Nectorama perfume by Tuvache—were selected for their power to draw customers to the supermarket, where they would fill out entry forms and maybe pick up some canned peaches. Most contestants were undoubtedly hoping for the grand prize, a piece of property and a furnished A-frame vacation home, already constructed and open for viewing at sites in the San Bernardino Mountains and at Lake Tahoe.[12]

A-FRAMES IN ADS

Raffles and sweepstakes offered free admission to a world of postwar leisure, fun, success, and pleasure. In the process they provided sponsors an opportunity to associate an event or product with that world by means of the A-frame. The multitude of advertisements featuring A-frame imagery intended similar connections. Often the goods being sold were directly related to the vacation home market. Second-home owners needed a collection of products with which to outfit their new homes, so the presence of an A-frame in ads for mini fridges and prefabricated fireplaces made perfect sense. By showing an appliance within an A-frame, advertisers suggested how well suited their products were to the second home. The A-frame was shorthand, establishing the location as one where leisure pursuits were played out, where style was up-to-date, where people wanted to be. In 1968 the Crane Company published an ad that featured its galley kitchen tucked neatly in the corner of an A-frame interior. Ads for Heatilator Brand prefabricated fireplaces showed a drawing of how the "chill-killing" design was particularly well adapted to "atticless homes or a typical A-frame's construction."[13] The makers of plastic-finished hardboard paneling, water pumps, cedar-shake panels, and a gas-fired "combustion toilet" called the

Gas-powered toilets were perfect for remotely located A-frame vacation homes, 1968

Destroilet all worked A-frames into their promotions. No other vacation home design was so instantly recognizable and unambiguous in its connection to the leisure lifestyle.[14]

Consumption did not stop with the outfitted vacation home. There were many other accessories necessary for postwar recreation. Was an A-frame vacation home complete without the playthings that made for a truly modern leisure life? If you had a snowmobile, you needed a vacation home. If you had a vacation home, where was your snowmobile? Widely available for the first time, aluminum- or plastic-hulled boats and off-road vehicles were as liberating as the private vacation home. They allowed their owners easy access to places outside established vacation areas and beyond the crowds.

Johnson Motors, manufacturer of outboard engines, powerboats, and snowmobiles, linked its products to the second home market by developing designs and advertisements that featured A-frames. A 1958 plan, published in *House & Garden*, drew the connection clearly:

*How to ski
sitting down –
on purpose*

Start something new!

Take 100% blue eyes in a field of blonde excitement... a sunlit Yamaha afternoon... a secluded rendezvous... clear out of sight... a wild scene! Yamaha gets you there with the grooviest off-the-road bikes anywhere. She looks great on the Trailmaster 100, and you're in full charge on the new Big Bear 305. Trailmaster goes with adjustable rear shocks, electric starter, speed breaker and quick-change dual sprocket. The Big Bear is built for the experienced rider, offers high pipes, startling torque, a top end in the neighborhood of 100 and has the looks of a man's bike. Check 'em out at your Yamaha Dealer's... the newest line-up in sportscycling... all race-bred from champions... safety engineered. And Yamaha warranties everything...everything except the girl.

For additional information or a copy of "Getting Serious for Safe Sportscycling," contact your nearest Yamaha Dealer or write: P.O. Box 54540, Los Angeles, Calif. 90054, Dept. PB B-1. Canadian Distributor: Yamaha Division of Fred Deeley Ltd., British Columbia.

YAMAHA ☼
INTERNATIONAL CORPORATION • SINCE 1887

"Boating, swimming, skin diving, water skiing, fishing and cruising are how you want to spend your days at lake or seashore and a good vacation house leaves you free to do just that." Designed for the "amphibious family," the A-frame was surrounded by a large wood deck and dock—with storage for skis and fishing gear—and adorned with a mast and boating flags. An exterior door to the bathroom helped keep sand outside, and a hinged roof panel could be raised during favorable weather, blending interior and exterior and allowing a view of the water-skiers from the couch.[15]

Ten years later Johnson Motors made a subtler attempt to co-opt the triangular structure in a *Field & Stream* advertisement for its snowmobile line. The ad showed Santa Claus abandoning his sleigh in favor of a Skee-horse. In the background lay the unmistakable shingled roof of an A-frame.[16] In 1967 Yamaha set a cross-gable A-frame behind a young couple in its ad for a new line of motorcycles that appeared in *Playboy* magazine.[17] Showing the demographic range of the structure's appeal, Yamaha did not target families seeking a base for outdoor vacations, but young bachelors who could appreciate a "secluded rendezvous" with "100% blue eyes in a field of blond excitement."

A-FRAMES IN THE YARD

In the spring of 1963 Malcolm VerNooy visited the Pompton Lakes Building Supply Company near his home in Wayne, New Jersey. VerNooy, a marketing manager for Union Carbide Chemicals Company, stopped in to pick up some redwood timber and plywood for a project he was planning for the next several weekends. At the sales counter, he saw an entry blank for a contest, sponsored by the Simpson Timber Company, asking participants to send in design ideas that used redwood. He filled out the form,

TOP **An A-frame in the background of this Johnson ad signals the location and atmosphere in which snowmobiling took place;** BOTTOM **A pair of Yamaha motorcycles, a girl, and a cross-gable A-frame appealed to *Playboy's* readers in 1967.**

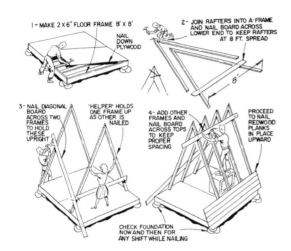

LEFT **Malcolm VerNooy's A-frame was easily assembled by Mom and Dad in a couple weekends, from Simpson Timber Company promotional material, 1964;** RIGHT **The VerNooy children and their mini vacation home**

describing his project: a backyard A-frame playhouse for his two children.[18]

VerNooy recalled years later that it was a "back-of-the-envelope kind of design."[19] He wanted to build a different sort of playhouse, unusual but also easy to construct. With ten-foot-long two-by-four rafters, an eight-by-eight-foot interior, and a second-level sundeck (which, like Dr. Hellyer's version, was reached by an exterior ladder) ,the playhouse was a scale model of a full-size A-frame vacation home. VerNooy spent about two months of weekends building it.

Simpson brought in some big names to judge the contest. In the end, designer Paul Laszlo; Louis Naidorf, vice president of Welton Beckett & Associates, Architects; and Frank Roodman, vice president of a major construction company, selected VerNooy's A-frame. The prize was a one thousand dollar bill. In exchange, VerNooy agreed to share his design with Simpson and permit the timber company to

reproduce it in ads and promotional articles.[20] A Simpson representative visited VerNooy's backyard, took photographs of the house, measured it, and drew up plans. Press releases announcing the contest results were first mailed to more than thirty newspapers, clipping bureaus, and radio stations in New Jersey and New York. In 1964 articles about the playhouse appeared in national magazines, including *Science and Mechanics*, *Home Maintenance and Improvement*, and *Mechanix Illustrated*.

Thanks to its frequent use by Bay Area designers and the energetic boosterism of the California Redwood Association, redwood was already closely tied to the trend of new architectural expressions that included the A-frame. Still, VerNooy's triangular playhouse was fortuitous for Simpson. By awarding the design first prize, the company claimed a relationship between its timber and the A-frame. Articles "based on materials supplied by the Simpson

Playhouse side of Richard Tyler's backyard A-frame, with a loft over the storage area, Edgewood, Indiana, 1962 Chicago Historical Society, HB-25807, photographs by Giovanni Suter, Hedrich-Blessing

Storage shed side of Tyler's A-frame

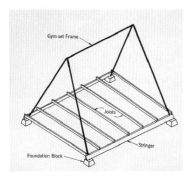

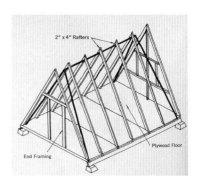

Playhouse built by Robert E. Watkins, featured in *Sunset* magazine, San Mateo, California, 1966; TOP CENTER Watkins reused the pipe frame of an old swingset.

Timber Company" emphasized the correlation with typical copy, which read: "The striking graciousness of this A-frame playhouse is enhanced by the beauty and ruggedness of the redwood used to build it."[21] The company also hoped that it was only a small leap in the customer's mind from a playhouse to a full-size vacation home.

VerNooy's backyard A-frame was no aberration. In 1965 *Popular Mechanics* ran an A-frame tree house on its June cover.[22] The accompanying article showed the house built atop the stump of a hurricane-felled tree. With the upper portions of the gable ends open, the design was essentially a balcony with a roof. A month later *Popular Science* countered with an equally stripped-down design in which the bottom half of the gable ends were left unfinished. Built by Carroll Daniels in Penn Yan, New York, for his grandchildren, the playhouse featured a full loft set over a concrete slab and built-in sandbox. It was made with plywood sheathing and diamond-shaped asphalt shingles over a row of two-by-four frames. According to the *Popular Science* author, the various colored shingles, leftovers from previous projects, gave a "Disneyland effect" to the house.[23]

The following year, in 1966, no less than four additional A-frame playhouses appeared in major American magazines, just a small sample

LEFT *Sunset* magazine featured this A-frame greenhouse in a 1950 article and 1960 gardening book
RIGHT A-frame outhouse, photograph from Bureau of Land Management files, 1960s

of the hundreds or thousands built to less fanfare. Essentially elaborate craft projects, the houses used the same materials as full-size structures, from four-by-eight-foot plywood sheets to red-cedar shingles.[24] They were usually designed by individuals who had no greater intention than bringing pleasure to their children or grandchildren. The number of individual A-frame playhouses built without the persuasion or plans of a major company suggests how far the idea had worked its way into popular culture.

Playhouses for kids could also be playhouses (or greenhouses or outhouses) for parents. In an article about Malcolm VerNooy's A-frame, *Mechanix Illustrated* proposed many other uses for the structure: "a workshop, ceramics studio, mini warehouse for storage, a hideaway for artist or author."[25] In 1962 Richard Tyler of Edgewood, Indiana, went halfway with a dual-use backyard A-frame. It was a schizophrenic structure, with separate entrances beneath each gable; one side was a storage shed and workshop, the other a playhouse for his kids.[26] Carroll Daniels's A-frame

was converted to a toolshed after his grandchildren outgrew it.[27] Weyerhaeuser Company offered plans in 1960 for an A-frame garden shelter and workbench in its free brochure series, "Fascinating Ideas."[28] Five years later Simpson Timber Company promoted a redwood backyard rec room.[29] *Sunset* magazine also offered alternative uses for the A-frame. As early as 1959 the magazine featured a redwood and plastic-sheet A-frame greenhouse and an equilateral triangle doghouse, complete with a glazed gable end.[30]

In a way, A-frame toolsheds and even doghouses brought the A-frame full circle, back to the utilitarian functions that the structure had been associated with since ancient times. As in the past, practicality was a primary motive for selecting the triangular form—it was quick, cheap, easy, and strong—but a desire to participate in the A-frame trend was also a factor. For many amateur builders, backyard projects were as far as their skills (or pocketbooks) could take them. Why build something boring?

A-FRAME DOLLHOUSES

Carrying miniaturization a step further, A-frame dollhouses began to appear during this period. Some were handmade, using scaled-down trusses to form a framework just like a full-size A-frame. Some were based on plans readily available in do-it-yourself books, newspapers, and craft and popular magazines.[31] Others were developed by major toy companies and sold in stores, complete and ready for imaginary vacations and pretend recreation.

Omlie Industries of Utica, Michigan, sold a toy A-frame ski cabin in the mid-1960s. Marketed "for all dolls," its proportions conveniently matched those of Mattel's hugely popular Barbie doll. A collection of straight plastic sheets (like little structural sandwich panels) slotted into angled corners to function as both roof and floor surfaces. Open gable ends provided ample access to an interior sparsely decorated with a couch, easy chair, coffee table, and fireplace. It was a decidedly modern interpretation of the A-frame, well suited to an urbane career woman like Barbie.

For children who identified with a more traditional version of the triangular vacation home, there was Fisher-Price's Play Family A-Frame. Developed by company designer Walter Doe, it was first unveiled at the International Toy Fair in New York City at the late date of 1974. Before designing the house, Doe sent away for plans of several full-size A-frames.

Picking and choosing among various elements, he formed a composite design, reconciled it with the requirements of a dollhouse, and succeeded in creating a fairly realistic interpretation of an A-frame vacation home.[32] To allow access to the two-story interior, he cut out most of one side of the roof, inserting a hinged door that, when open, functioned as a patio. It was a solution that the designers of full-size A-frames, working around the dark inner recesses of an unaltered triangular building, probably wished they could employ.[33] The package, which originally sold for six dollars, included the house, a family of four "little people," a car, a pair of chaise lounges, benches, a ladder to reach the upper-level sleeping space, two sets of bunk beds, and a table with lithographs depicting a sizzling steak, just arrived from the grill.

When Fisher-Price decided to release a vacation home dollhouse, the rational choice was to base it on an A-frame design.[34] When any company wanted to secure a place in the leisure market, it could do so with A-frame imagery and promotions. By the early 1970s, the triangular form needed no explanation. As one of the plan books noted, "the popularity of the A-frame has made this type of structure a symbol to many people of stylish contemporary living in the carefree manner."[35] And though this iconic status would continue for decades to come, the A-frame's popularity could not last forever.

ABOVE **Omlie Industries modern A-frame dollhouse;** BELOW **Vinyl dollhouse by Ideal Toy Company, 1971**

Fisher-Price Little People Play Family A-frame advertisement, 1974

The Fisher-Price A-Frame

4 bunk beds

Fireplace

Built-in kitchen

4-passenger jeep

Sliding doors

2 deck chairs

Dinner bell

Fold-out terrace

Picnic table
2 benches

2 chairs
Barbecue grill

This charming vacation house with twin balconies, twin decks,
sleeping loft and dining terrace is the setting for four Play Family People
and their dog to have fun.
Enroute, all the pieces fit inside, the terrace folds up into the roof,
and snaps shut to form a carrying handle.

© 1974 Fisher-Price Toys, East Aurora, New York 14052. Division of The Quaker Oats Company.

Conclusion

A-frame: A Conclusion

As the 1960s turned into the 1970s, the A-frame began a gentle fall from its preeminent place in postwar vacation home design. At the same time, the number of new A-frame churches, shops, restaurants, and motels rapidly decreased. Developers and prefabricators that had specialized in A-frame vacation homes went out of business or switched to newer models. *Sunset* and *House Beautiful* moved on to the next big thing. Though new A-frame construction dwindled, its influence on subsequent vacation, and even permanent, home design trends continued, and its place in the popular conception of recreation architecture remained undiminished. Even today the triangular house, more than any other structure, conjures up images of leisure and the good life.

The A-frame's decline followed the trajectory of most modest vacation homes during the period. Designs that were small in scale, short on amenities, and based on playful forms—designs that reflected a democratization of leisure life and the optimism of the postwar period—were out of step when some of that optimism proved unfounded. Changing tastes and fading fashion played a part. With tens of thousands of A-frames scattered across the country, the design lost some of its whimsical, eye-catching allure. It was not unexpected to see them at recreation areas and resorts from coast to coast and around the world. To some, the A-frame was a spent trend, an idea whose time had passed.

VACATION HOME BUST

At the end of the 1960s the vacation home market reached a new level of maturity and diversification. In addition to individual homes on isolated lots, consumers could choose among condominiums, time-share programs, houseboats,

A-frame off Route 20 near Galena, Illinois

and mobile homes. Planned resort communities had become increasingly popular as the decade progressed. Signaling a shift in what people wanted from their leisure hours, vacation communities provided all the comforts of a permanent residence in a semicontrived natural setting. With streets of vacation homes surrounding a clubhouse, marina, private beach, or ski lift, these developments were more like suburban subdivisions than rustic retreats. In some ways, they marked a return to the nineteenth-century upper-class vacations spent at resort hotels, where socializing and being seen were the main agenda. One banker speculated that, despite all the rhetoric about outdoor recreation and escape, "city people don't really want to be alone. They get panicky when they see trees."[1]

Because these communities required large initial investments in roads, sewers, clubhouses, and marinas, they also signaled a shift away from the small-scale projects by individual entrepreneurs that characterized earlier vacation home developments. Forest-product companies moved from offering plans and kits to underwriting entire resort communities. They were joined by automakers, railroads, oil companies, movie studios, and other deep-pocketed investors interested in broadening their holdings and getting a piece of what seemed like an endless demand for recreation.[2]

Optimistic economic forecasts, aggressive promotion campaigns, and liberal lending policies nudged individuals to purchase vacation properties throughout the 1960s. Income generated by subletting the house when it was not in use helped cover what would otherwise have been an unaffordable second home mortgage. Investors and owners prospered when demand exceeded the supply of vacation homes. Beginning in 1970, though, it was increasingly a renter's market, when second home owners scrambled to find tenants, and recreation community house lots lay unclaimed. Explanations for the downturn included the growing popularity of "motor-driven campers" and "the general economic situation—high interest rates, diminished fortunes in the stock market, growing layoffs, and rising unemployment."[3] Potential buyers were further discouraged by tax code changes that eliminated the second home as a financial shelter, a series of land speculation scandals, and a shortage of quality recreation lots.[4]

Two decades of unrestricted vacation home and outdoor recreation-related construction had done considerable damage to the landscapes that many sought to escape to. Once discovered—or opened to access by new roads—idyllic, isolated vacation spots quickly attracted company. By the early 1970s, an increasingly assertive environmental movement was taking aim at some of the more egregious developments and sought passage of land-use regulations that limited where new homes could be built. As a result, prime recreation land grew scarcer and more expensive.[5]

An energy crisis in 1973 only exacerbated the difficulties facing the second home market.[6] The postwar vacation home boom and the designs that accompanied it were predicated on cheap and plentiful fuel. As the cost of heating oil and gasoline lurched upward, fewer could afford the drive to a place in the country and to keep such places heated in the winter. With thin roofs, single-glazed gable ends, and two-story living rooms, typical A-frames—particularly those in remote locations—were not well poised to ride out the hard times.

The new economic realities squeezed modest designs and many middle-class families

Zippy the Pinhead laments the passing of A-frames and cantilevers from commercial architecture, 2000

out of the second home market. Condos and time-shares became a preferred option for those of more moderate means, who might have built their own triangular house a few years before. The increasing cost of desirable recreation property made eight-thousand-dollar A-frames anachronistic. Those who could afford the land and were not dissuaded by the interest rates and energy bills turned to more substantial designs, complete with full-size kitchen, washer and dryer, and garage. In the decades ahead, architects and owners gradually retreated from the whimsy and experimentation that had characterized the contemporary vacation home. Today, there is little to distinguish vacation homes from permanent homes; the distinction between a place to live and a place to play has largely disappeared. The spirit of experimentation has also faded from commercial architecture. Fast food restaurants and other businesses replaced loud colors, surprising angles, and contorted roofs with simulated stucco and watered-down historicism.

"THE SILLIEST FAD..."

By 1970, the A-frame vacation home had been around for more than twenty years. No longer bold and brash, its seeming ubiquity at recreation areas made it commonplace and almost cliché. *Business Week* wrote of "rank on rank of A-frame cottages marching into infinity."[7] A 1968 cartoon that ran in *Ski* magazine summed up the worn-out attitude toward the A-frame. Attempting to escape a typical downhill resort, the intrepid skier completes a journey to the other side of the world, only to find identical runs, leading down to an identical cross-gabled A-frame, in Afghanistan.[8]

Throughout its run, affection for the triangular vacation home was not unanimous. One real estate agent I spoke with recalled a client who, several years after buying an A-frame, told him, "The next time I buy a house, by God, it's going to have walls!"[9] Judging, though, by the number of A-frames that were owned for decades by the same family, many more were

"Ski Life" cartoon by Bob Cram, 1968

satisfied with their odd-shaped homes. After all, they were only occupied for a weekend, or a week at a time. During this time, the fun and quirks must have outweighed the occasional bump on the head, the cramped quarters, and the lack of privacy. It would be interesting to know if those who lived—or live—in A-frames year-round agree or share the sentiments of the young English girl who thought that "Teapot Hall was the worst of all."[10]

From the publication of Wally Reemelin's Berkeley Duplex to the mid-1970s vacation home bust, there were surprisingly few published criticisms of the A-frame. Whether through self-interest or genuine affection, magazine editors and guide book authors were nearly unanimous in their praise. There were a few detractors, though. As early as 1964, one author wrote, "The silliest fad I have seen lately are those ultra-steep roofs which come all the way to the ground. If they were intended to rear above the snow on a picturesque mountaintop, I might get the point, but I couldn't design a structure which would give you less interior space for your money."[11]

That same year, a *Ski* magazine editorial by architect Alan Liddle lamented not the impracticality of A-frame structures, but their appearance. According to Liddle, they were part of a larger problem with American ski resort architecture, which he described as "a chaotic conglomeration to behold—A-frames with scallops and carved shutters, imitation Swiss chalets with sliding aluminum doors and tarpaper roofs, stuccoed plywood Hofbrau Hauses with murals painted on the second story overhangs, pink log cabins ablaze with neon. We are aping stylistic facades that the sophisticated foreigner has rejected decades ago." Liddle blamed "the overall eclectic state of contempo-rary American architecture," as well as speculative developers and a lack of an American mountain building tradition.[12]

Liddle's criticism, at least as far as the A-frame was concerned, was off the mark. He called for a mountain architecture that fulfilled the rugged demands of an Alpine climate, that was "informal and casual, uncomplicated but imaginative," that was sensitive to the site and allowed nature to dominate. They were the very attributes that so many people saw in the A-frame. Liddle wanted architecture that fit these requirements "within a contemporary idiom without resorting to old-worldism," exactly the achievement of many A-frame designs.[13] For every A-frame with a yodeling porch, there was a subtler design that successfully integrated the traditional triangular form with contemporary features.

As the A-frame became less popular, vacationers were less willing to put up with its shortcomings. Variations that went beyond dormers and inset walls appeared with increasing frequency. Some were attracted to the "modified A-frame" with a mansard roof that, instead of joining at the peak, ended at a more gently sloping secondary pitch or a flat roof. Although it provided more head room and wasted less space than an equilateral A-frame, dormers and inset walls were awkward and usually left out of a modified design. As a result, these modified versions were usually more cardlike than triangular ones.[14] The increasing appearance of knee walls at the base of the sloping roof marked another departure from the pure A-frame. By placing a vertical wall along the lower three or four feet of the structure, the roof was raised sufficiently to not be of concern, even in the loft area, and appliances and furniture could be placed directly against the interior walls. Like

"Modified A-frames" enjoyed a brief popularity as designers sought to update the form, Squaw Valley, 2003 photograph

the mansard, these designs retained the glass gable ends made so popular by the A-frame.

During the vacation home boom, the triangular form was widely adopted for both avant-garde designs and the most rudimentary do-it-yourself shacks. It traversed economic and social boundaries, explaining, in part, why they were so useful to advertisers and promoters. From the 1970s on, however, the A-frame lost its association with high-style living and was increasingly considered a lowbrow housing type, perhaps because it was no longer so distinctive or because it was seen as undersize and amateur-built. Maybe the A-frame liquor stores and car washes along commercial strips were to blame. Most likely, it was just the aftertaste of a faded fashion. This prejudice continues today, as A-frame motels are relegated to the budget traveler and A-frame homes are considered quaint but dated, cramped, and a bit tacky.

There was no clearly defined moment when the triangular vacation home slipped from prominence. In 1972 author Chuck Crandall claimed that "vacation homes are no longer A-frames built from plans snipped out of *Popular Mechanics*" and that the market and potential buyers had moved on.[15] Yet the following year, as if to counter Crandall's assessment, *Popular Mechanics* published plans for two A-frames, one of which was featured on the issue's cover.[16] Throughout the 1970s and after the vacation home market rebounded in the 1980s, A-frames were still being built. But the attention these designs received was vestigial and inconsequential compared with the preceding decades. Though it disappeared from magazine covers, exhibitions, and advertisements, the A-frame did survive—in the stock of homes built during the boom years, in the new A-frames still occasionally built, and in the still visible influence the form exerted on wider architectural circles.

LASTING IMPACTS

Some of the most provocative postwar architecture was designed for leisure living. Small size, low cost, and freedom from the requirements of

**Vista Springs model, by
Lindal Cedar Homes, 2003**

a permanent home encouraged a spirit of experimentation and a willingness to explore the unorthodox. The A-frame was a catalyst for this trend, as well as one of its best examples. The triangular vacation home broadened the thinking of postwar leisure seekers. It blended into the landscape in which it was built, accommodated the desire to escape everyday life, and opened the door to an "anything goes" attitude toward recreational design, the repercussions of which were felt beyond the beach and mountainside.

The two A-frame characteristics most appreciated by vacationers were the glazed gable end and the full-height main living room with an upper level loft behind. The glass wall directed attention outward and filled the interior with light. The living room, where most indoor waking hours were spent, was a dramatic and flexible space, with the view and the fireplace forming perpendicular focal points. Upstairs, the loft provided an informal, tree house-like sleeping space, and access to the sunlight and view was provided through the gable end. These features quickly made their way into other contemporary vacation home designs; eventually they showed up in permanent homes as well.

In 1967 Jerry Shapiro, the developer of a New Jersey resort called Beach Haven West, said, "Once vacation homes were little more than inadequate, smaller versions of the family's permanent home. Now the second home is the source of design innovations for permanent homes. Design concepts first pioneered by builders in second home communities have been adapted to the winter home."[17] Thumb through plan books from the last thirty years and it's easy to spot the A-frame's influence. Prow-shaped glass walls are set beneath steeply pitched gables. Inside, glass walls almost invariably front a large central living area that has a second level loft at the back. Even today, the A-frame's lines can be discerned in many contemporary year-round and vacation homes. Lindal Cedar Homes, a major A-frame kit producer in the 1960s and now a leading home manufacturer, has several designs with two-story glass prows and bedroom lofts that overlook a main living area and expansive deck. Suggestive of the company's own involvement in the A-frame form, these designs are part of the Classic Home series.

Portions of the cement block fireplace and garage walls were all that survived of Betty Reese's A-frame, 1962

SURVIVING POSTWAR A-FRAMES

Whether influential or not, A-frames from the 1950s to the 1970s are still around: vacationers are still renting them, tired travelers are still pulling over to catch some sleep in triangular motels, hot dogs and six-packs are still handed through A-frame drive-through windows, and congregations still gather in A-frame churches. Triangular structures used by businesses to attract customers still dot roadsides and resort areas, often having long outlasted the companies that built them. An A-frame liquor store turned into an A-frame fabric store, which was later converted into an A-frame pet shop. Howard Johnson still has some cross-gabled A-frame offices. But, as if embarrassed, they have been remodeled to disguise their original form. At locations that Howard Johnson sold or that went out of business, new motels have opened with as little alteration as a coat of paint over the orange roof and a new sign out front. Wienerschnitzel and Whataburger still have A-frame buildings in service. To this day the triangular shape is relied upon to suggest something worth pulling over the car to see.

A-frame churches, not susceptible to the vagaries of roadside commerce, vacancies, and rerouted highway interchanges, seem to have fared better than A-frame businesses. Saarinen's Kramer Chapel is lovingly cared for by Concordia Theological Seminary. Additions and alterations are made to triangular churches, but most congregations continue to appreciate them and to find them conducive to worship. New A-frame churches occasionally appear, not from the ground up but through the conversion of existing A-frames. In 2000 the African Baptist Church of North Dallas had outgrown its rented space in a nearby church. The congregation, which included immigrants from five African countries, Jamaica, and Canada, needed its own building. The pastor, Paul Franka, recalled, "We started praying and asking God to show us where to go." The Lord showed them a Whataburger. They purchased the vacant restaurant, removed the large steel W from the exterior, installed chairs and a small pulpit, and started services.[18]

Most of the houses built as part of the first wave of architect-designed A-frames have sur-

Dr. David Hellyer and his A-frame, 2003

vived to today. Wally Reemelin's triangular houses can be found perched on the hills above Berkeley. Although a little worn and in need of paint, their views across the San Francisco Bay obscured by trees, they are in good structural shape and largely unaltered. On the other side of the country and almost as old, the A-frame designed by Henrik Bull is still owned by his college roommate, John Flender. Less fortunate was Betty Reese's Long Island A-frame, designed by Andrew Geller. Despite the structure's presumed invincibility, the Reese House succumbed to a winter storm in 1962. Fortunately, because the house was so similar to Geller's A-frame for Leonard Frisbie and because the Frisbie House has been largely untouched by remodeling campaigns, it is still possible, in a way, to experience the Reese House.

There are no longer any six-hundred-square-foot vacation homes in the neighborhood where John Campbell built his 1952 Leisure House. Mill Valley, California, is now a pricey bedroom community in one of the wealthiest

counties in the country. Converted to a permanent home soon after he sold it in the mid-1950s, Campbell's A-frame has been altered and expanded beyond recognition. In fact, a couple of floor joists are the only original pieces to survive.

Dr. Hellyer's A-frame continues to stand on the pebbly beach at Henderson Inlet, in Washington state. Designed and constructed by the physician-naturalist-builder in 1957, the house remains structurally sound but somewhat the worse for wear. It is still easily recognizable as the DFPA's twenty-year-long promotional vehicle, its image reproduced in a hundred articles and its plan mailed out by the tens of thousands.

The four-by-eight-foot plywood "shingles" are still on the roof, though they are now beneath subsequent layers of asphalt shingles and wood shakes. New grooved panels were installed over the original Texture One-Eleven siding, and a single window has replaced the paired awning windows on the second-floor gable end. Outriggers that once extended from the second level deck have been sliced off, as

One of Wally Reemelin's Berkeley A-frames in 2003

has the ladder to the upper deck and the principal rafters crossing at the roof peak. The exposed rafter on the side of the building with inset vertical walls was removed at some point, upsetting the triangular form and throwing the building off balance. Though individually these features are minor, when missing, their collective importance to the design is obvious. With Hellyer's thoughtful details stripped from the exterior, it now seems nondescript, as if fifty years of the coming and going tide rubbed away what made it great. Fortunately, the plan bore many offspring, some of which survive, some of which are brand new.

And what of the tens of thousands of other A-frames that followed? Much depended upon their location, as postwar A-frames often sit on land that is much more valuable than the modest structures themselves. One bedroom A-frames near Lake Tahoe—which were built in the 1960s for around ten thousand dollars, including the lot—regularly list for between three hundred thousand and four hundred thousand dollars. They are a steal in an area where most vacation homes are at least half a million dollars and ten-million-plus properties are not unheard of. A 2002 *Forbes* magazine article noted that the average sale price in Aspen, another site of early A-frame construction, was more than 3.5 million dollars that year.[19]

But it isn't just home prices that distinguish the current vacation home market from that of the A-frame's era. From the 1950s to the 1970s, the A-frame, and other second homes, represented an escape from the everyday life of careers and conformity. They were sites for brief escapes, otherworldly places where one could hide out for short periods of stripped-down living before returning to the rat race. This had changed by 2002, when the *New York Times*

ABOVE **Perlman House in 2003;** TOP RIGHT
**Adriene Biondo and John Eng's house,
Idyllwild, California, 2003;** BELOW RIGHT **Tony
Russomanno's A-frame at Lake Tahoe, 2003**

observed that "instead of traditional lakeside chalets, newcomers are seeking out big houses in the countryside—typically colonial styles that can double as primary residences if work schedules can be juggled." The paper called the term *second home* obsolete, as city dwellers had come to view vacation homes as the center of their home lives.[20]

In this climate modest postwar A-frames just don't fit in. It is increasingly the rule that they are bought for the land beneath them and promptly demolished or enlarged beyond recognition.[21] The original A-frame, if it survives, is left to function as a bedroom, entryway, or mudroom. In either case, a new large home is the result. This is the fate that might befall the Rockrise A-frame in Squaw Valley, which was sold in 2003 to owners who, rumor had it, planned to build their own dream vacation home on the property. Despite being in excellent structural condition, almost entirely unaltered,

and one of the best surviving examples of the postwar A-frame vacation home, it is considered an obstacle.

Modest postwar A-frames seem to survive only in places where the recreation market has subsided and a city commute is out of the question. Sometimes a tenacious owner holds onto the property unchanged, or a new owner appreciates the cultural cache of the triangular house and works to preserve it. There are some A-frame enthusiasts today who, captivated by the spirit of postwar leisure, purchase A-frames and

remodel them with a mix of mid-century modern and contemporary furnishings. Adriene Biondo and John Eng were attracted to the A-frame not as a teardown, but as a rehabilitation project. They bought a triangular house in Idyllwild, California, not far from Palm Springs, and recently completed an interior and exterior remodeling. Tony Russomanno recently bought and restored an A-frame at Lake Tahoe. The A-frame constructed in the 1960s by vacation home builder Peter Hack is a "Hack Shack." Russomanno is currently compiling a history of Hack and his company, Thomas Construction. [22]

NEW A-FRAMES TODAY

While some are saving old A-frames, others are constructing new ones. Confirming the A-frame's continued cultural potency, architect Steven Izenour of Venturi, Scott Brown and Associates built one on Mount Desert Island, Maine. Constructed in 1998, the building serves as a library and sculpture studio for the Acadia Summer Arts Program. Also known as Kamp Kippy, after its founder Marion "Kippy" Stroud, the fellowship program sponsors a season of independent work, interaction, and relaxation for artists, critics, and museum administrators. The A-frame was based on vacation houses and motels the architect passed on frequent trips between Portland and Bar Harbor, Maine; Izenour's version, however, came out quite differently. While Maine is best known for shingled fishing villages and picturesque lighthouses, Izenour found inspiration in other indigenous forms: "big lobster signs, A-frame cabins, trailers, lawn ornaments, and old cars and tractors rusting on the edge of blueberry fields." [23] The result was a triangular building that is both unlike any other and just like every other.

The Kamp Kippy A-frame is an explicit capital *A*, with a horizontal cross member on the main facade, separating the entrance from a triangular window above. Familiar vernacular materials were used throughout—clapboard siding, divided light windows, and a standing-seam metal roof. The language of the roadside—including bold, attention-getting colors, pink flamingos, big-butt gardeners, and a cutout-letter sign—was amplified and accentuated throughout.

Izenour's A-frame pays homage to Maine's everyday architecture. It is the ordinary made extraordinary, it acknowledges the intersection of sign, symbol, ornament, and architecture as central cultural communicators of the American landscape. By making them emphatic, the building playfully encourages a reappraisal of what "people of 'good taste' love to hate." It strives to recapture some of the whimsy that was attached to the A-frame during its boom years yet is essentially an affirmation that the popular conception of the A-frame today is of an unexceptional, lowbrow building form. In a 1998 newspaper interview shortly before his death, Izenour recalled, "When Kippy said she planned to build several art studios here, I immediately thought of an A-frame. It is the most under-appreciated architectural form."[24]

Though in far fewer numbers, A-frame plans can still be found today, interspersed with the neotraditional bungalows and cottages that crowd plan books and plan-service Internet sites. Some of the designs look very familiar. As of May 2003, plans for David Hellyer's A-frame were available for purchase on an Internet web site for U-bild. A well-known supplier of do-it-yourself woodworking plans and kits, U-bild offered the drawings for $9.95. To depict the completed project, the company included one of the photographs taken by DFPA in 1957. A U-bild representative reported that the company sells hundreds of these plans each year.[25]

Larry Stover bought a set. In 2001 he was searching on the Internet for vacation home plans for his lot on the Green Briar River in West Virginia. "Ever since I was a boy, I've been intrigued by the A-frame," Stover said, but he was hesitant to build one, considering the interiors too dark and cramped. When he saw Dr. Hellyer's A-frame on the U-bild site, with its inset windows lighting the center of the house and two deck levels, he changed his mind and ordered the plans. His goal was to build as nice a home as possible as cheaply as possible. With some construction experience, Stover was the foreman. He picked up stock windows, got a deal on some metal roofing, and set to work over a weeklong vacation with his crew of three brothers-in-law: a minister, a retired postal worker, and a banker. While Hellyer's A-frame

OPPOSITE **Steven Izenour's design of the A-frame for Arts was inspired by this A-frame in West Gouldsboro, Maine;** ABOVE **A-frame for Arts, Mount Desert Island, Maine, 1998**

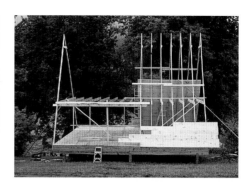

Construction of Larry Stover's A-frame, using David Hellyer's plans, Hinton, West Virgina, 2002

was a plywood paradise, Stover skipped the material altogether; he preferred knotty pine. Because the roof is not insulated, the sheathing doubled as an interior surface.

Stover selected an A-frame design for many of the reasons discussed in this book. Though rooted in traditional building forms, it seemed an appropriate setting for recreational activities and the passing of leisure time. The A-frame was distinctly different from everyday architecture; it exhibited a harmony with nature, blurred the distinction between interior and exterior, could be built by the nonprofessional, and was cheap. The A-frame boom has come and gone, yet tens of thousands of A-frames still dot the landscape, and they still attract attention. As Stover was finishing up the work on his A-frame, a passing car slowed and pulled over to the side of the road. An old man stuck his head out the window and said, "When are you going to build a house under that roof?"

Leisure-time

CABINS

#4   A-FRAME BEACH CABIN

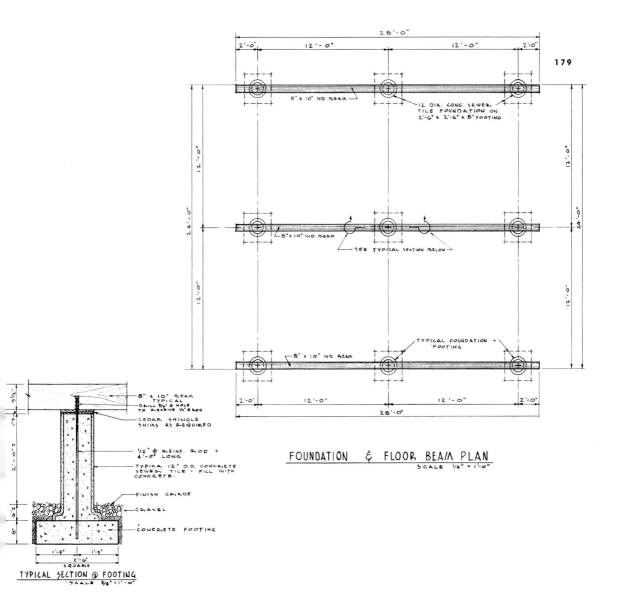

28'-0"

2'-0"   12'-0"   12'-0"   2'-0"

8" X 10" WD. BEAM

12" DIA. CONC. SEWER
TILE FOUNDATION ON
2'-6" X 2'-6" X 8" FOOTING

12'-0"

24'-0"

8" X 10" WD. BEAM

SEE TYPICAL SECTION BELOW

12'-0"

TYPICAL FOUNDATION +
FOOTING

8" X 10" WD. BEAM

2'-0"   12'-0"   12'-0"   2'-0"

28'-0"

FOUNDATION & FLOOR BEAM PLAN
SCALE 1/4" = 1'-0"

8" X 10" BEAM
TYPICAL
DRILL 3/4" Ø HOLE
TO RECEIVE 1/2" ROD

CEDAR SHINGLE
SHIMS AS REQUIRED

1/2" Ø REINF. ROD X
4'-0" LONG

TYPICAL 12" O.D. CONCRETE
SEWER TILE - FILL WITH
CONCRETE.

FINISH GRADE

GRAVEL

CONCRETE FOOTING

1'-3"   1'-3"

2'-0"
SQUARE

TYPICAL SECTION @ FOOTING
SCALE 3/4" = 1'-0"

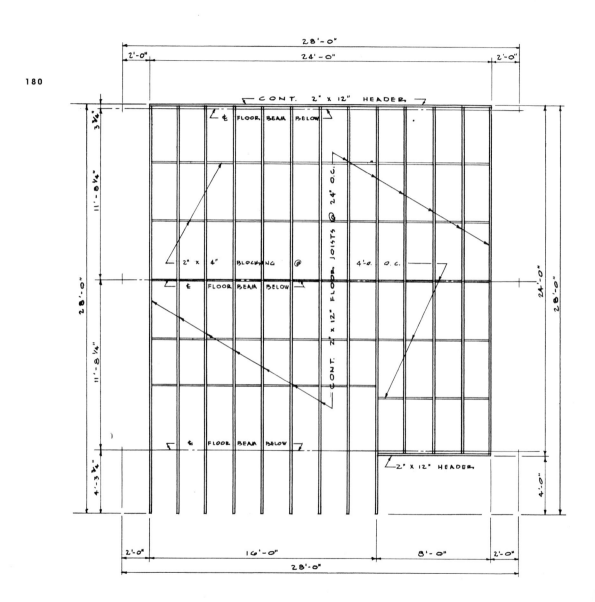

CONT. 2" X 12" HEADER

₵ FLOOR BEAM BELOW

2" X 4" BLOCKING @ 4'-0. O.C.

CONT. 2" X 12" FLOOR JOISTS @ 24" O.C.

₵ FLOOR BEAM BELOW

₵ FLOOR BEAM BELOW

2" X 12" HEADER

28'-0"

2'-0"   24'-0"   2'-0"

3 ¾"

11'-8¼"

28'-0"

11'-8¼"

4'-3¾"

24'-0"

28'-0"

24'-0"

4'-0"

2'-0"   16'-0"   8'-0"   2'-0"

28'-0"

FIRST FLOOR & DECK FRAMING PLAN

SCALE : 1/4" = 1'-0"

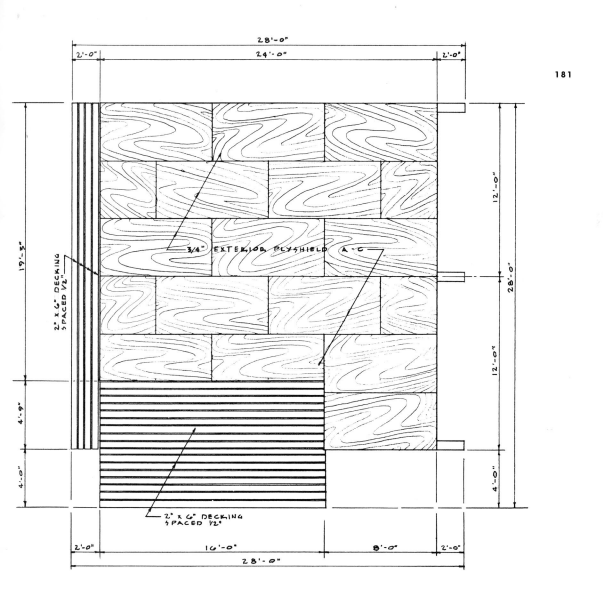

3/4" EXTERIOR PLYSHIELD A-C

2" x 6" DECKING
SPACED 1/2"

2" x 6" DECKING
SPACED 1/2"

28'-0"

24'-0"

2'-0"

2'-0"

19'-3"

12'-0"

28'-0"

12'-0"

4'-9"

4'-0"

4'-0"

2'-0"

16'-0"

8'-0"

2'-0"

28'-0"

FIRST FLOOR & DECK FINISH PLAN
SCALE 1/4" = 1'-0"

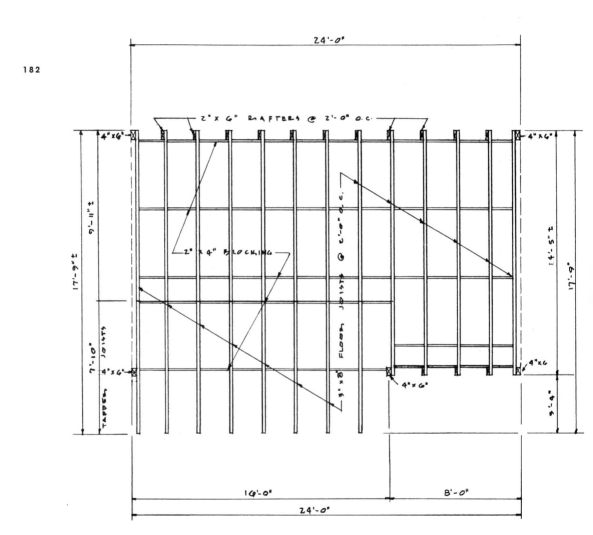

SECOND FLOOR & DECK FRAMING PLAN

SCALE 1/4" = 1'-0"

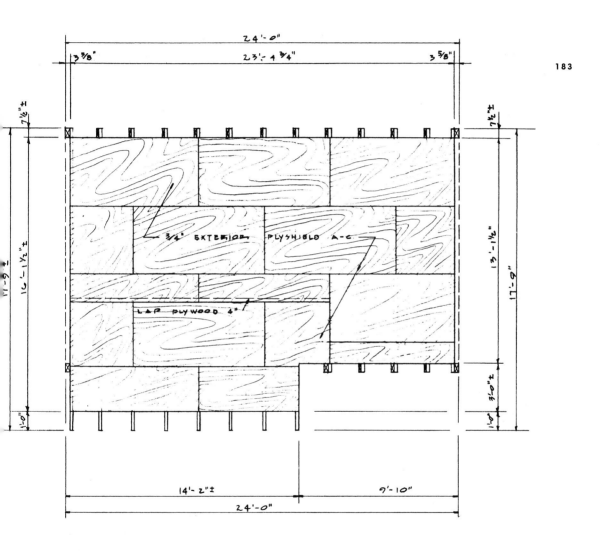

SECOND FLOOR & DECK FINISH PLAN

SCALE ¼" = 1'-0"

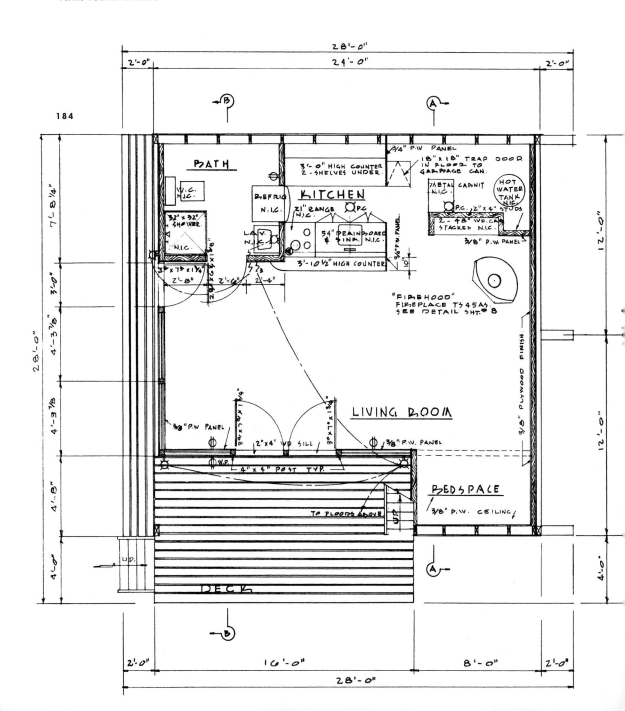

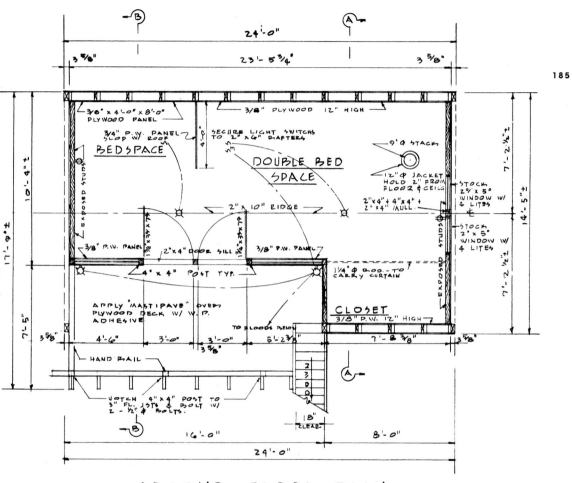

24'-0"
23'-5 3/4"
3 5/8"
3 5/8"

3/8" x 4'-0" x 8'-0"
PLYWOOD PANEL

3/8" PLYWOOD 12" HIGH

3/4" P.W. PANEL
SLOP W/ ROOF

SECURE LIGHT SWITCHES
TO 2" x 6" RAFTERS

9"Ø STACK

BEDSPACE

DOUBLE BED
SPACE

12"Ø JACKET
HOLD 2" FROM
FLOOR & CEILG

STOCK
2'9" x 5'0
WINDOW W/
4 LITES

2" x 10" RIDGE

2" x 4" + 4" x 4" +
2" x 4" /WALL

EXPOSED STUDS

3/8" P.W. PANEL

2" x 4" DOOR SILL

3/8" P.W. PANEL

STOCK
2' x 5'
WINDOW W/
4 LITES

4" x 4" POST TYP.

1 1/4"Ø ROD.-TO
CARRY CURTAIN

EXPOSED STUDS

APPLY "MASTIPAVE" OVER
PLYWOOD DECK W/ W.P.
ADHESIVE

CLOSET
3/8" P.W. 12" HIGH

TO FLOORS BELOW

HAND RAIL

4'-6"
3'-0"
3'-0"
3 5/8"
5'-2 3/8"
7'-8 3/8"
3 5/8"

NOTCH 4" x 4" POST TO
3" FL. JSTS & BOLT W/
2 - 1/2"Ø BOLTS.

2
3
0
1

18"
CLEAR

16'-0"
8'-0"

24'-0"

10'-4" ±
17'-9" ±
7'-5"
3 5/8"

7'-2 1/2" ±
14'-5" ±
7'-2 1/2" ±

SECOND FLOOR PLAN
SCALE 1/4" = 1'-0"

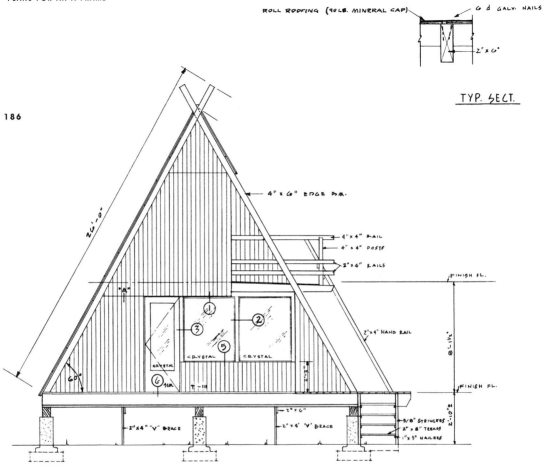

ROLL ROOFING (90 LB. MINERAL CAP)   6 d GALV. NAILS

2" X 6"

TYP. SECT.

186

4" x 6" EDGE BM.

4" x 4" RAIL
4" x 4" POSTS
2" x 4" RAILS

FINISH FL.

2" x 4" HAND RAIL

8'-1½"

FINISH FL.

26'-0"

"A"

① ②
③
⑤

CRYSTAL   CRYSTAL
CRYSTAL

⑥ SIM
T-1-11

60°

2" x 6"

2" x 4" "V" BRACE
2" x 4" "V" BRACE

3/8" STRINGERS
2" x 8" TREADS
1" x 3" NAILERS

2'-10"

LEFT   ELEVATION
SCALE ¼" = 1'-0"

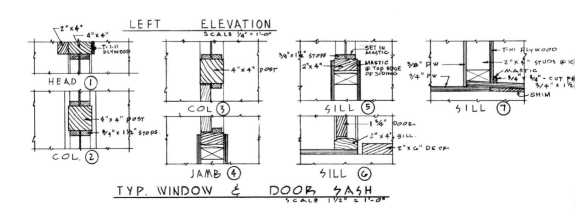

2" x 4"
4" x 4"
T-1-11 PLYWOOD

HEAD ①

4" x 4" POST
3/4" x 1½" STOPS.

COL. ②

4" x 4" POST

COL ③

JAMB ④

3/4" x 1½" STOPS
2" x 4"
SET IN MASTIC
MASTIC @ TOP EDGE OF SIDING

SILL ⑤

1¾" DOOR
2" x 4" SILL
2" x 6" DECK

SILL ⑥

T-1-11 PLYWOOD
2" x 4" STUDS @ 16
3/8" PW
3/4" PW
3/4" - CUT PW
3/4" x 1½"
SHIM

SILL ⑦

TYP. WINDOW & DOOR SASH
SCALE 1½" = 1'-0"

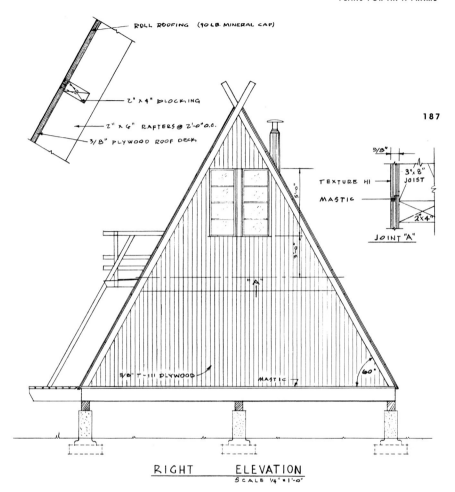

ROLL ROOFING (90 LB. MINERAL CAP)

2" x 4" BLOCKING

2" x 6" RAFTERS @ 2'-0" O.C.

3/8" PLYWOOD ROOF DECK

TEXTURE HI

MASTIC

3/8"

3" x 8" JOIST

2" x 4"

JOINT "A"

"A"

5/8" T-111 PLYWOOD

MASTIC

60°

RIGHT   ELEVATION
SCALE 1/4" = 1'-0"

DESIGN NOTE

This cabin has been designed throughout for maximum construction economy. In order to accomplish this so that more people can afford adequate vacation homes, it utilizes a "direct plywood roof." That is – plywood panels are used as giant shingles exposed directly to the weather. Naturally, the degree of watertightness of such a roof depends upon the quality of application, workmanship and joint sealers used. Since the application of this type of roof can not be supervised, no liability for its watertightness can be assumed by the designer. However, if your cabin program is guided by extreme economy you should take advantage of the quality roof sheathing base provided by plywood construction and either now, or later when your financial outlook has improved, permanent roofing (wood or asphalt shingles, shakes, roll roofing) can be installed over the plywood sheathing.

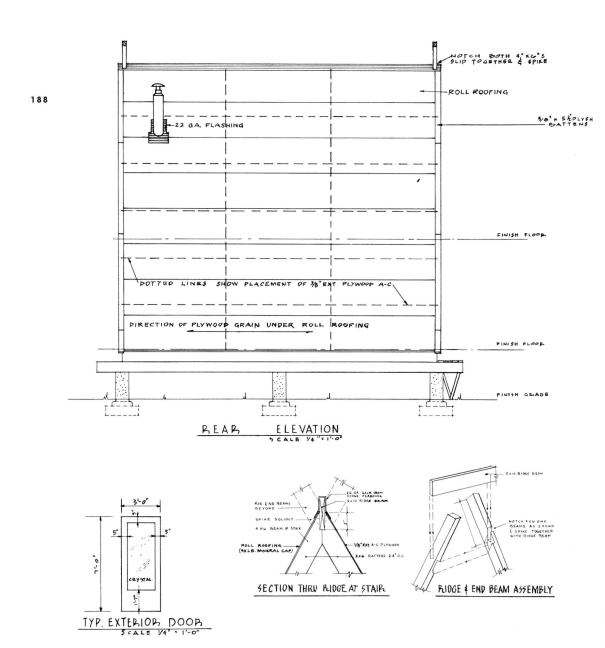

NOTCH BOTH 4"x6"S
SLIP TOGETHER & SPIKE

ROLL ROOFING

3/8" x 5½" PLYSH
BATTENS

22 GA. FLASHING

FINISH FLOOR

DOTTED LINES SHOW PLACEMENT OF 3/8" EXT PLYWOOD A-C

DIRECTION OF PLYWOOD GRAIN UNDER ROLL ROOFING

FINISH FLOOR

FINISH GRADE

REAR ELEVATION
SCALE ¼" = 1'-0"

3'-0"

5"   5"

7'-0"

CRYSTAL

TYP. EXTERIOR DOOR
SCALE ¼" = 1'-0"

26 GA GALV IRON
RIDGE FLASHING
2x10 RIDGE BEAM

4x6 END BEAMS
BEYOND

SPIKE SOLIDLY

4x6 BEAM @ STAIR

ROLL ROOFING
(90 LB. MINERAL CAP)

3/8" EXT A-C PLYWOOD

2x6 RAFTERS 24" O.C.

SECTION THRU RIDGE AT STAIR

2x10 RIDGE BEAM

NOTCH 4x6 END
BEAMS AS SHOWN
& SPIKE TOGETHER
WITH RIDGE BEAM

RIDGE & END BEAM ASSEMBLY

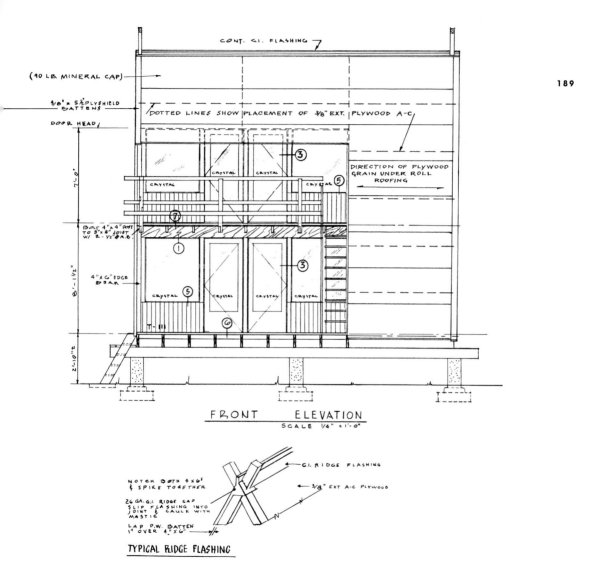

CONT. G.I. FLASHING

(90 LB. MINERAL CAP)

3/8" x 5½"PLYSHIELD BATTENS

DOOR HEAD

DOTTED LINES SHOW PLACEMENT OF 3/8" EXT. PLYWOOD A-C

DIRECTION OF PLYWOOD GRAIN UNDER ROLL ROOFING

CRYSTAL   CRYSTAL
CRYSTAL   CRYSTAL

BOLT 4"x 4" POST TO 3"x 8" JOIST W/ 2- ½" Ø M.B.

4"x 6" EDGE BEAM

CRYSTAL   CRYSTAL   CRYSTAL   CRYSTAL

7'-0"

8'-1½"

2'-0"

FRONT   ELEVATION
SCALE ¼" = 1'-0"

NOTCH BOTH 4x6's & SPIKE TOGETHER

26 GA. G.I. RIDGE CAP SLIP FLASHING INTO JOINT & CAULK WITH MASTIC

LAP P.W. BATTEN 1" OVER 4" X 6"

G.I. RIDGE FLASHING

3/8" EXT A-C PLYWOOD

TYPICAL RIDGE FLASHING

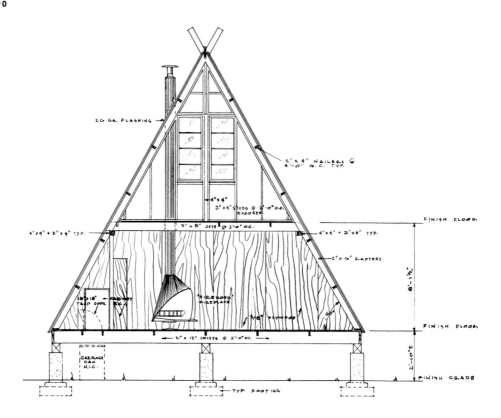

26 GA. FLASHING

2" x 4" NAILERS @
4'-0" O.C. TYP.

4" x 4"
2" x 4" STUDS @ 2'-0" O.C.
EXPOSED

FINISH FLOOR.

4" x 4" + 2" x 4" TYP.

3" x 8" JSTS @ 2'-0" O.C.

4" x 4" + 2" x 4" TYP.

2" x 6" RAFTERS

18"x18"
TRAP DOOR

CABINET
ETC.

FIREHOOD
FIREPLACE

3/4" PLYWOOD

8'-1½"

GARBAGE
CAN N.I.C.

2" x 12" JOISTS @ 2'-0" O.C.

FINISH FLOOR.

2'-10½"

TYP. FOOTING

FINISH GRADE

SECTION "A-A"
SCALE ¼" = 1'-0"

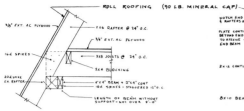

2ⁿᵈ FLOOR JOIST TO RAFTER CONNECTION

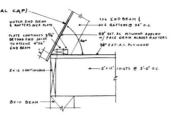

1ˢᵀ FLOOR JOIST TO RAFTER CONNECTION

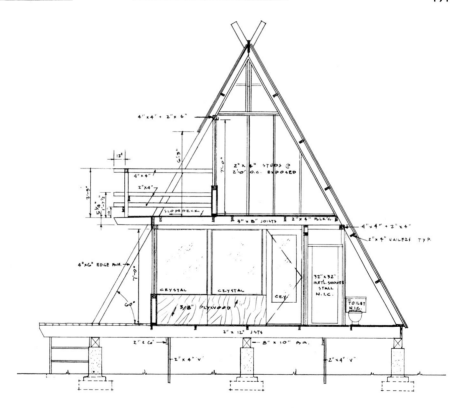

SECTION "B-B"
SCALE 1/4" = 1'-0"

192

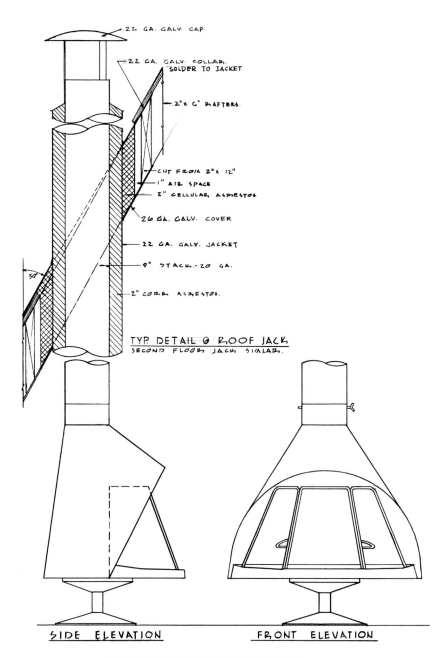

22 GA. GALV. CAP.

22 GA. GALV. COLLAR.
SOLDER TO JACKET

2" x 6" RAFTERS.

CUT FROM 2" x 12"
1" AIR SPACE
2" CELLULAR ASBESTOS

26 GA. GALV. COVER

22 GA. GALV. JACKET

9" STACK - 20 GA.

2" CORR. ASBESTOS.

30

TYP. DETAIL @ ROOF JACK
SECOND FLOOR JACK SIMILAR.

SIDE ELEVATION

FRONT ELEVATION

FIREPLACE DETAILS

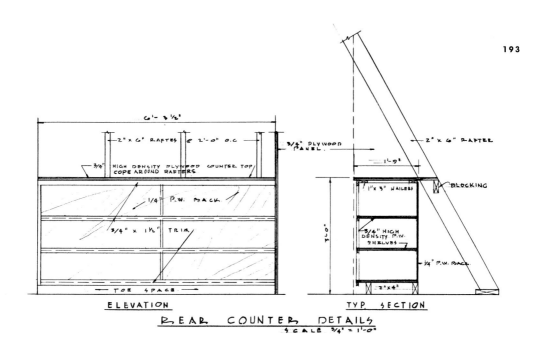

2" x 6" RAFTER @ 2'-0" O.C.

3/4" PLYWOOD PANEL.

3/4" HIGH DENSITY PLYWOOD COUNTER TOP.
COPE AROUND RAFTERS

1/4" P.W. BACK

3/4" x 1½" TRIM

TOE SPACE

6'- 3 ½"

ELEVATION

2" x 6" RAFTER

1'-9"

BLOCKING

1" x 3" NAILERS

3/4" HIGH DENSITY P.W. SHELVES

1/4" P.W. BACK

2" x 4"

3'-0"

TYP. SECTION

REAR COUNTER DETAILS

SCALE 3/4" = 1'-0"

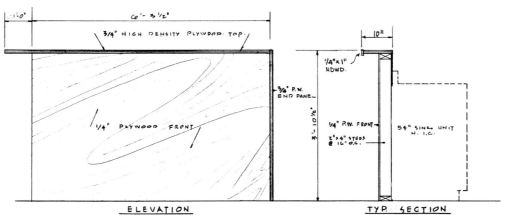

6'- 3 ½"

3/4" HIGH DENSITY PLYWOOD TOP.

3/4" P.W. END PANEL.

1/4" PLYWOOD FRONT

ELEVATION

10"

1/4" x 1" HDWD.

1/4" P.W. FRONT

2" x 4" STUDS @ 16" O.C.

54" SINK UNIT N.I.C.

3'- 10½"

TYP. SECTION

FRONT COUNTER DETAILS

SCALE 3/4" = 1'-0"

MATERIALS   LIST

	USE	MATERIAL
PLYWOOD	FLOORING (FIRST & SECOND FLOOR)	EXTERIOR A-C
	TEXTURE ONE – ELEVEN SIDING	PATTERN 48/4
	ROOF + BATTENS	EXTERIOR A-C
	INTERIOR WALL PANELING	INTERIOR A-D
	KITCHEN COUNTER TOP + SHELVES	HIGH DENSITY EXTERIOR PLYW
	KITCHEN COUNTER FRONT + BACK	INTERIOR A-D
	KITCHEN COUNTER , STANDARDS + BOTTOM	INTERIOR A-D
FRAMING LUMBER DOUGLAS FIR OR HEMLOCK	FLOOR BEAMS	NO. I SELECT STRUCTURAL
	FIRST FLOOR FRAMING	NO. I FRAMING
	SECOND FLOOR FRAMING	NO. I FRAMING
	SECOND FLOOR FRAMING BEAMS	NO. I FRAMING
	ROOF FRAMING - EDGE BEAMS	NO. I FRAMING
	RAFTERS	NO. I FRAMING
	RIDGE BEAM	NO. I FRAMING
	PLATES , STUDS, BLOCKING & NAILERS +STEPS	NO. 2 & BETTER
	DECKING	NO. 2 & BETTER
FINISH LUMBER, DOORS & WINDOWS DOUGLAS FIR OR PINE	WINDOW & DOOR FRAMES + HAND RAILS	NO. I DIMENSION
	WINDOW & DOOR STOPS	V. G. FIR OR PINE
	KITCHEN CABINET FRAMING	NO. 2 DIMENSION
	INTERIOR DOOR	HOLLOW CORE
	EXTERIOR DOORS	SOLID CORE W/ LITE
	STOCK WINDOWS	V. G. FIR OR PINE
MASONRY	FOUNDATION PADS	CAST - IN- PLACE
	FOUNDATION SEWER TILE	PRECAST CONCRETE
	STAIR FOUNDATION PADS	CAST -IN – PLACE
ROUGH HARDWARE	MACHINE BOLTS	STEEL
	NAILS	
	NAILS	
	NAILS	
	NAILS	GALV. OR ALUMINUM
FINISH HARDWARE	EXTERIOR & INTERIOR DOOR BUTTS	STEEL US 26 D FINISH
	EXTERIOR LOCK SETS	
	INTERIOR BATHROOM LATCH	
MISCELLANEOUS	GLAZING	CRYSTAL SHEET
	RIDGE FLASHING	26 GA. G.I.
	MASTIC	NON – DRYING
	FIBERGLASS MEMBRANE OVERLAY OR SYNTHETIC RUBBER MEMBRANE	DECK COVERING
	STEEL ROD	STEEL
	FIREPLACE – "FIREHOOD" TS 45 AS	STEEL
	INTERIOR & EXTERIOR FINISH	STAIN OR PAINT
	ROLL ROOFING	90 LB. MINERAL CAP

SIZE	QUANTITY	REMARKS
3/4" X 4'-0" X 8'-0"	28 SHEETS	
5/8" X 4'-0" X 8'-0" + 10'-0"	16 SHEETS	INCLUDES 4 SHEETS @ 10'-0"
3/8" X 4'-0" X 8'-0"	33 SHEETS	
3/4" X 4'-0" X 8'-0"	2 SHEETS	
3/8" X 4'-0" X 8'-0"	19 SHEETS	
3/4" X 4'-0" X 8'-0"	2 SHEETS	
1/4" X 4'-0" X 8'-0"	2 SHEETS	
3/4" X 4'-0" X 8'-0"	2 SHEETS	

SIZE	QUANTITY		REMARKS
8" X 10" - 3 AT 28'	84 L.F.	560 B.F.	
2" X 12" - 9 AT 28' , 4 AT 24'	348 L.F.		
- 4 AT 8'	32 L.F.	750 B.F.	
3" X 8" - 8 AT 18' , 5 AT 16'	224 L.F.	416 B.F.	
4" X 4" - 12 AT 8'	96 L.F.	128 B.F.	
4" X 6" - 5 AT 26'	130 L.F.	275 B.F.	
2" X 6" - 18 AT 24' , 8 AT 8'	497 L.F.	496 B.F.	
2" X 10" - 1 AT 24'	24 L.F.	40 B.F.	
2" X 8" - 7 AT 8'	56 L.F.	72 B.F.	
2" X 4" - 154 AT 8'	1226 L.F	816 B.F.	
2" X 6" - 20 AT 16' , 8 AT 12'	416 L.F	416 B.F.	

SIZE	QUANTITY		REMARKS
2" X 4" - 10 AT 8'	80 L.F.	52 B.F.	
4" X 4" - 10 AT 8'	80 L.F	104 B.F.	
3/4" X 1 1/2"	320 L.F.		
1" X 3"	30 L.F.		
2'-8" X 6'-8" X 1 3/8"	1 REQUIRED		
3'-0" X 7'-0" X 1 3/4"	5 REQUIRED		GLAZE W/ CRYSTAL
2'-0" X 5'-0"	2 REQUIRED		4 LITES , GLAZE W/ CRYSTAL

SIZE	QUANTITY	REMARKS
2'-6" X 2'-6" X 8"	9 REQUIRED	
12" X 36"	9 REQUIRED	FILL W/ CONCRETE
3'-0" X 2'-0" X 4"	1 REQUIRED	

SIZE	QUANTITY	REMARKS
1/2" X 5"	6 REQUIRED	
6, 8 & 16 d COMMON	AS REQUIRED	FRAMING, FLOORING & DECKING
4, 6 & 8 d COMMON	AS REQUIRED	MILLWORK & INTERIOR PANELING
8 d CONCRETE	AS REQUIRED	STAIRS TO FOUNDATION
6 d BOX OR CASING	AS REQUIRED	SIDING & ROOF PANELS

SIZE	QUANTITY	REMARKS
4" X 4" LOOSE PIN	6 PAIR	
AS REQUIRED	5 REQUIRED	
STANDARD	1 REQUIRED	

SIZE	QUANTITY	REMARKS
JOB MEASURE - APPROX. 60" X 48"	6 REQUIRED	STOPPED IN PER DETAIL
AS DETAILED	24 L.F.	
	AS REQUIRED	AT LAPS, BATTENS, GLAZING & JOINTS
	AS REQUIRED	COVER UPPER EXTERIOR DECK
1/2" ⌀ X 4'-0"	9 REQUIRED	
45"	1 REQUIRED	MANUFACTURED BY "CONDON-KING CO."
	AS REQUIRED	1247 RAINER AVE.
		SEATTLE 44, WASHINGTON
24" ROLLS	AS REQUIRED	

NOTES: APPLIANCES & FIXTURES (PROVIDE AT EXTRA COST)
  APPLIANCES & FIXTURES, IF INSTALLED, SHALL MEET LOCAL & STATE CODES IF APPLICABLE.
  FIREPLACE TO BE INSTALLED TO MEET ALL LOCAL & STATE CODES IF APPLICABLE

  EXTERIOR PAINTING AREAS (WALLS, ROOF & DOORS + DECKS)   1450 SQ. FT. APPROX.
  INTERIOR PAINTING AREAS (PANELING, CEILING, FLOORS, STUDS & ROOF) 3300 SQ. FT. APPROX

INTRODUCTION

1 Douglas Fir Plywood Association, "Every Family Needs Two Homes," promotional banner (Tacoma, Wash.: Douglas Fir Plywood Association, c. 1962).

2 Structures with roof rafters that do not continue all the way to the floor but are interrupted by vertical knee walls do not retain the basic triangular shape and therefore are not considered A-frames.

3 Of the few architectural style guides that mention the A-frame, Lester Walker's *American Shelter* is the most comprehensive. His book posits seven different types of A-frame. Three (the standard, double standard or cross-gable, and A-frame with wings) fit within the definition used for this study. Walker's arched A-frame, gambrel-roof A-frame, and flat-top A-frame are not triangular in form. *American Shelter: An Illustrated Encyclopedia of the American Home* (Woodstock, N.Y.: Overlook Press, 1981), 250. These field guides and illustrated dictionaries provide an interesting perspective on the challenges of classifying postwar architecture. When the A-frame is included it is often categorized as "contemporary folk" housing. (See Virginia McAlester and Lee McAlester, *A Field Guide to American Houses*, New York: Knopf, 1984, 497.) As chapter one discusses, the triangular building form had once been part of many vernacular building traditions, passed down from one generation to the next. However, many postwar versions, including those discussed in chapter three, were professionally designed exercises in engineered geometry. While amateur-built triangular vacation homes certainly were an important part of the A-frame boom, their design was inspired by mass-culture vehicles, like national magazines, rather than tradition.

CHAPTER 1

1 See Sheldon M. Gallager, "Why the Big Boom in A-frames?" *Popular Science*, August, 1961, 128.

2 "Summer Shelters," *Look*, 20 May 1952, 74.

3 "A-frame: Ultra-Modern 'Tepee,'" *Pittsburgh Press*, 7 July 1963, sec. 6, p. 1.

4 Skin or fabric-covered conical shelters that date to the Upper Paleolithic period and survived as tepees and yurts do not figure into this discussion. Circular rather than rectilinear in plan, they were not considered permanent structures but, rather, were designed by nomadic cultures for quick construction and disassembly. This is not to say that such shelters did not inspire affection for the A-frame on the part of some designers and owners.

5 See Jack Bowyer, *History of Building* (London: Crosby, Lockwood and Staples, 1973); and, more recently, G. R. H. Wright, *Ancient Building Technology*, vol.1, *Historical Background* (Boston: Brill, 2000). The early theories of building

prehistory were speculation, unhindered by lack of evidence and colored by aesthetic controversies of the day. Other hypotheses, including that of Viollet-le-Duc, had primitive builders weaving together branches leaned against upright trees. Perhaps unintentionally close to the mark, the result would have resembled the conical or spherical woven-grass houses discussed in several contemporary studies of Ethiopian and African building traditions. See Eugène-Emmanuel Viollet-le-Duc, *The Habitations of Man in All Ages*, trans. Benjamin Bucknall (Ann Arbor, Mich.: Gryphon Books, 1971), 5; and Naigzy Gebremedhin, "Some Traditional Types of Housing in Ethiopia," in *Shelter in Africa*, ed. Paul Oliver (London: Barrie & Jenkins, 1971), 10.

6 Ronald G. Knapp, *China's Traditional Rural Architecture* (Honolulu: University of Hawaii Press, 1986), 6.

7 Japanese architectural ideas had an important impact on American postwar design along the West Coast and on vacation homes in particular. Discussing this "new architecture of leisure," *Sports Illustrated* writer Cranston Jones observed that "since the Japanese have traditionally been great believers in bringing nature into the house and projecting the house into nature, it is not surprising that some age-old Japanese solutions have appealed to indoor-outdoor living Americans." Although the A-frame was not among the solutions Jones discussed, it reflected in many ways the Japanese approach to architecture and the construction of some of Japan's earliest shelters. See Cranston Jones, "The New Architecture of Leisure," *Sports Illustrated*, 14 January 1963, 37.

8 Jiro Harada, *The Lesson of Japanese Architecture* (Boston: Charles T. Branford, 1954), 14. See also A. L. Sadler, *A Short History of Japanese Architecture* (Rutland, Vt.: Charles E. Tuttle, 1963); and Atsushi Ueda, *The Inner Harmony of the Japanese House* (Tokyo: Kodansha, 1998). The *tenchi-kongen tsukuri* design was almost identical to the tong-support structure's precursor, as described by C. F. Innocent.

9 In *The Inner Harmony of the Japanese House*, Atsushi Ueda argues that the pillars supporting the roof had, in addition to their structural importance, a central symbolic importance.

10 Bruno Taut, *Houses and People of Japan*, 2nd ed. (Tokyo: Sanseido, 1958), 132–133. Taut theorized that the farmhouse design was a remnant of a "finer, lighter and more versatile spirit of an earlier Japan" that had been crushed by a succession of military dictatorships that, the author intimated, continued to the present (the first edition of Taut's book was published in 1937).

11 Ronald Lewcock and Gerald Brans, "The Boat as an Architectural Symbol," in *Shelter, Sign and Symbol*, ed. Paul Oliver (London: Barrie &

Jenkins, 1975), 107. Lewcock and Brans suggested that these forms were probable descendants of early Japanese and Chinese triangular building forms, also originally boat symbols. Most Americans' exposure to Pacific architecture was through the stylized tiki restaurants and resorts that proliferated during a mid-century fling with all things "Polynesian." Attention on World War II's Pacific theater, the atomic testing at Bikini, and the admission of Hawaii as the fiftieth state in 1959 led to an American fascination and titillation with South Pacific culture, from luaus and pineapples to hula dancing and mai-tais. In some cases there was little to distinguish tiki restaurant forms from all-roof A-frames. See Sven A. Kirsten, *The Book of Tiki: The Cult of Polynesian Pop in Fifties America* (Los Angeles: Taschen, 2003).

12 The tong support may have been a progression from even earlier inverted V-shaped huts whose ridgepoles were supported not by a pair of inclined timbers but by a row of vertical posts with forked ends, which cradled the ridgepole. Rafters were then leaned against the ridgepole along the length of the structure. The shift in favor of tong-support frames likely came about because of their superior strength, the placement of a doorway in the middle of the gable end, and a more open floor plan free of central supports. See C. F. Innocent, *Development of English Building Construction* (London: Cambridge University Press, 1916), 23.

13 James Walton, "Development of the Cruck Framework," *Antiquity* 22 (1948): 179.

14 Innocent, *Development of English*, 23.

15 Sigurd Erixon, *Svensk Byggnadskultur* (Stockholm: Aktiebolaget Bokverk, 1947), 68.

16 Innocent, *Development of English*, 27.

17 Dorothy Hartley and Margaret M. Elliot, *Life and Work of the People of England in the Fourteenth Century* (London: G. P. Putnam's Sons, 1925), pl. 26 f. "The Romance of Alexander," MS 264, pt. 1 fol. 204r, Bodleian Library, Oxford University.

18 With the availability of curved, glue-laminated wood beams in the years following World War II, framework similar to cruck construction came into use again, particularly for gyms, auditoriums, and farm buildings. In 1971 *Sunset* magazine's book *Cabins and Vacation Houses* contained plans for an A-frame variation based on such glue-lam beams. See Sunset's *Cabins and Vacation Houses* (Menlo Park, Calif.: Lane Book Company, 1971), 7.

19 Barbara A. Hanawalt, *The Ties That Bound* (New York: Oxford University Press, 1986), 35. Structures built with either crucks or tong-supports could, like later A-frames, be extended in length indefinitely by simply adding rows of rafters.

20 N. W. Alcock, "The Definition of a Cruck," in *Cruck Construction: An Introduction and*

Catalog, ed. N. W. Alcock (London: Council for British Archaeology, 1981), 4.

21 Much of the information about Teapot Hall can be found in John Constable, "The Tale of Teapot Hall," *Lincolnshire Life*, May 2002.

22 Kathleen Wood lived in the house for four years with her parents and three siblings. Though they are perhaps the earliest surviving reminiscence from an inhabitant of a triangular structure, Wood's sentiments must have been shared by previous all-roof building dwellers and were identified again when the A-frame vacation home emerged during the postwar period.

23 A. A. Milne, *The Complete Tales of Winnie-the-Pooh* (New York: Dutton Children's Books, 1994), 183. [From the Complete Tales of Winnie-the-Pooh by A. A. Milne, illustrated by E. H. Shepard. This presentation copyright © 1994 by Dutton Children's Books. Coloring of the illustration copyright © 1992 by Dutton Children's Books. *The House at Pooh Corner* by A. A. Milne, illustrated by E. H. Shepard, copyright © 1928 by E. P. Dutton & Co., Inc.; copyright renewal 1956 by A. A. Milne. Used by permission of Dutton Children's Books, a division of Penguin Young Readers Group, a member of Penguin Group (USA) Inc., 345 Hudson St., New York, NY 10014. All Rights Reserved.]

24 Gun Schönbeck, "Victor von Gegerfelt: Arkitekt i Göteborg" [Architect in Gothenburg] (Ph.D. diss., University of Gothenburg, 1991), 260.

25 Victor von Gegerfelt, "En Saga Om Bâd Gammel Och Nywulna Hus" [A Saga of Some Old and Recent Buildings] (Gothenburg, Sweden: Regionarkivet Region-och Stadsarkivet, 2000). This manuscript is held by the city and county council archives in Gothenburg, Sweden.

26 Walton, "Development of the Cruck," 179.

27 Innocent, *Development of English*, 25.

28 Robert Woods Kennedy, *The House and the Art of Its Design* (New York: Reinhold, 1953), 341. The photo is reproduced in Kennedy's book with a caption noting that a client had cut the photo from *Life*'s pages and added it to a scrapbook. The book was an assembly of ideas for a future home that would provide "a maximum of wall surface on which to hang pictures." The scrapbook also included R. M. Schindler's Lake Arrowhead cabin for Gisela Bennati.

29 May intended his "self-help" A-frames to be constructed with semiskilled labor, using factory-produced kits. He selected a triangular shape because it would be easy to build and considered acceptably vernacular in the conservative German countryside. Susan R. Henderson, "Ernst May and the Campaign to Resettle the Countryside: Rural Housing in Silesia, 1919–1925," *Journal of the Society of Architectural Historians*, June 2002, 203. Artaria's weekend cottage was built near Tessenberg, Switzerland, in the 1920s. Paul Artaria, *Vom Bauen und Wohnen* [Building and Living] (Basel,

Switzerland: Wepf & Co., 1948), 34. The A-frame hut by Carl Weidemeyer was built in Worpswede, Germany, in 1914. Bruno Maurer and Letizia Tedeschi, *Carl Weidemeyer: 1882–1976* (Mendrisio, Italy: Accademia di Architettura, 2001), 231.

30 G. E. Kidder, *Switzerland Builds: Its Native and Modern Architecture* (New York: Albert Bonnier, 1950), 81.

31 G. I. Meirion-Jones notes that it wasn't until the agrarian reforms that accompanied the establishment of the European Economic Community that the basic triangular shelter began to rapidly disappear from the French landscape. G. I. Meirion-Jones in *Cruck Construction*.

32 Dan Beard, "Some New Winter Camps, and How to Build Them and Heat Them," *Outing*, October 1904, 370.

33 David Hellyer, while working for a firm called Ski Lifts, Inc., built an A-frame shelter to cover the lift engine at Paradise Valley on Mount Rainier, in Washington state. Hellyer's A-frame vacation homes are discussed in chapter four. Dr. David T. Hellyer, interview by the author, Eatonville, Wash., 25 April 2003.

34 David Gebhard, *Schindler* (Santa Barbara, Calif.: Peregrine Smith, 1980), 62.

35 Fact sheet probably used as a press release, R. M. Schindler, 1934.

36 David Leclerc, "The Cave and the Tent: An Introduction to Schindler's Domestic Architecture," *Kenchiku Bunka* 54 (1999): 107.

37 Dominique Rouillard, *Building the Slope: Hillside Houses 1920–1960* (Santa Monica, Calif.: Arts and Architecture Press, 1987), 57.

38 It is unknown if contact with triangular structures during Schindler's youth in Austria played any role in his inspiration for the Bennati house. It is possible that decades before, as an architecture student in Vienna, he came across reference to Weidemeyer's hut or passed an unknown triangular cottage in the Alps. Perhaps as an expatriate in Los Angeles, keeping abreast of the artistic goings-on in his homeland, he read of Ernst May's or Paul Artaria's exploration of the form.

39 "Cabin for Gisela Bennati," *Arts and Architecture*, February 1944, 22.

40 Ibid., 21.

41 "A Weekend House in California," *The Architect's Journal*, 25 July 1946, 66.

42 Conrad Meinecke, *Your Cabin in the Woods* (Buffalo, N.Y.: Foster & Stewart, 1945).

CHAPTER 2

1 Nationwide, spending on leisure increased from approximately eight million dollars in 1946 to almost twenty-four million in less than twenty years. "Vacation Homes: An Exploding Market Takes On a New Shape," *House & Home*, February 1964, 107. The article states, "It is this

upward trend—product of rising incomes and more leisure—that underpins the expanding second-home market. The more consumers spend on recreation the more they are likely to consider a home where recreation is the focal point."

2 From a paper read at the Home Manufacturers' Association's 22nd Annual Convention, quoted in Richard Lee Ragatz, "The Vacation Home Market: An Analysis of the Spatial Distribution of Population on a Seasonal Basis, Volume I" (Ph.D. diss., Cornell University, 1969), 60.

3 Bill Osgerby, *Playboys in Paradise: Masculinity, Youth and Leisure-Style in Modern America* (New York: Berg, 2001), 81.

4 William J. Hennessey, *Vacation Houses* (New York: Harper and Row, 1962), vii.

5 In 1945 consumer credit was at 5.7 billion dollars, and by 1970 it had climbed to more than 143 billion dollars. During the early 1960s an expanding universal credit card industry was mass-mailing unsolicited charge cards, creating twenty-six million cardholders by the end of the decade. Though second homes were not financed on the cards, the refrigerators, hi-fis, rugs, and other furnishings used to stock them often were. See Lloyd Klein, *It's in the Cards: Consumer Credit and the American Experience* (Westport, Conn.: Praeger, 1999), 27; and Lewis Mandell, *The Credit Card Industry: A History* (Boston: Twayne, 1990), 35.

6 "A Vacation House Can Pay for Itself," *American Home*, July 1961, 72.

7 *Free-Time Homes*, 2nd ed. (Portland, Oreg.: Potlatch Forests, Inc., 1962), 21. Customers could buy a kit with no money down, using either a thirty-six-month payment plan to cover a portion of the cost or a five-to-seven-year mortgage plan for the entire price of the house.

8 Ragatz, "The Vacation Home Market," 46.

9 By 1968, the Bureau of Land Management had created more than two hundred reservoirs and more than ninety-five hundred miles of shoreline. Between its creation, in 1933, and 1968, the Tennessee Valley Authority created more than ten thousand miles of new shoreline, which accommodated at least twelve thousand vacation homes. See Clayne R. Jenson, *Outdoor Recreation in America* (Minneapolis: Burgess Publishing Co., 1970), 80, 88.

10 Ragatz, "The Vacation Home Market," 79.

11 Real estate and building trade magazines routinely discussed the distance an average family was willing to travel to reach its vacation home. As highways and reliance upon the automobile proliferated, that distance grew.

12 See John Jakle, Keith A. Sculle and Jefferson S. Rogers, *The Motel in America* (Baltimore: Johns Hopkins University Press, 1996).

13 There was some degree of recentralization

in the early 1970s, when increasing costs, the increasing scarcity of prime vacation property, and a decrease in labor-intensive second home ownership shifted purchases to the vacation community and condominium.

14 "A-frames: New Cabin Fever," *True: The Man's Magazine*, October 1959, 60.

15 *The Changing American Market*, by the editors of *Fortune* magazine (New York: Time, Inc., 1955); reprinted as "$30 Billion for Fun," in *Mass Leisure*, ed. Eric Larrabee and Rolf Meyersohn (Glencoe, Ill.: Free Press, 1958), 168. The piece also noted that the number of families earning more than four thousand dollars increased from twenty percent just before the Depression to more than forty-five percent by 1953. This statistic is especially important because many economists believed that when a family reached the four-thousand-dollar income level, they began to spend an increasingly larger portion of that income on leisure. *Fortune* called them "the rulers of the leisure market."

16 Predictions that by the year 2000 the average work week would be down to thirty hours and that most Americans would enjoy four weeks of paid vacation per year further pointed to a coming "crisis of leisure." See Paul F. Douglass and Robert W. Crawford, "Implementation of a Comprehensive Plan for the Wise Use of Leisure," in *Leisure in America: Blessing or Curse?*, ed. James C. Charlesworth (Philadelphia: American Academy of Political and Social Science, 1964), 55.

17 Quoted in Jensen, *Outdoor Recreation in America*, 5.

18 The emphasis on worthwhile leisure and its expression through family activities often reinforced traditional gender roles. Historian Elaine Tyler May borrowed Cold War political language in describing the response to the threat of communist expansion when she wrote that female sexuality and leisure were "contained" during this period, the former within the traditional family and the latter through constructive use of leisure. Elaine Tyler May, *Homeward Bound: American Families in the Cold War Era* (New York: Basic Books, 1988). The amount of work involved in second home ownership presents questions about how much vacation was had by the wife and mother. Imagery from the period is conflicting. Illustrations of women carrying trays of drinks to seated husbands are often adjacent to those showing tool-belted women participating in vacation home construction. Throughout the period modest contemporary vacation homes were touted as low maintenance, for the sake of both husband and wife.

19 "NAHB Spring Builder's Conference Report," *National Association of Home Builders Journal of Homebuilding*, May 1963, 14.

20 As one government report observed,
This use of leisure is important to the health of individuals and to the health of the nation. The physical vigor of a nation is as

much a part of its strength as good education. Even in this era of electronic warfare, men are still the key to vigilant defense. In many situations a fit man with a rifle in his hands is the only effective defense, and in those where machines are the combatants, fit men must direct them. The increasingly high rate of men rejected by the army for physical reasons—three of every seven called—together with the obvious benefits of good health to individuals argue eloquently for the better physical fitness that many forms of outdoor recreation provide.

See *Outdoor Recreation for America: A Report to the President and to Congress by the Outdoor Recreation Resources Review Commission* (Washington, D.C.: Government Printing Office, January 1962), 23. The Department of the Interior administered a "small tracts" program in which recreational lot sales went from 103 in 1951 to almost ten thousand in 1960. In that ten-year period more than forty-three thousand recreation lots were sold. "Vacation Cabins," *NAHB Journal*, August 1962, 61.

21 Office of Civil Defense Document *PSDC-TR-2 Expedient Community Shelter Semi-Buried A-frame*, U.S. Protective Structures Development Center, Joint Civil Defense Support Group, Office of the Chief of Engineers/Bureau of Yards and Docks, 13 May 1965; and Office of Civil Defense Document *PSDC-TR-10 Family Shelter A-frame*, same publisher, 8 October 1965.

22 Osgerby, *Playboys in Paradise*, 81.

23 Concerns over such activities were voiced in a 1961 exposé about cabins: "Winter 'athletes' set aside snowshoes and skiis [sic] while male-chasing females turn on the heat in pursuit of more intimate indoor sports—romance and wild parties." Gene Channing, "Sin in Snowland: The Shame of Ski Lodge Shack-ups," *Man's Life*, January 1961, 33.

24 "Modern Living: Do It Yourself," *Time*, 30 June 1952.

25 Albert Roland, "Do-it-Yourself: A Walden for the Millions," *American Quarterly*, Summer 1958, 162.

26 Steven M. Gelber, *Hobbies: Leisure and the Culture of Work in America* (New York: Columbia University Press, 1999), 276.

27 Roland, "Do-it-Yourself," 162.

28 Witold Rybczynski, *Waiting for the Weekend* (New York: Penguin, 1991), 173.

29 See *Redwood Vacation Homes* (San Francisco: California Redwood Association, 1930); *Log Cabins and Summer Cottages* (Newark, N.J.: Sears Roebuck & Co., 1940); Conrad Meinecke, *Your Cabin in the Woods* (Buffalo, N.Y.: Foster &

Stewart, 1945). During the postwar period log cabins were increasingly made from kits of log veneer. Thus a building form associated with American grit and self-reliance was relegated to mass production in a factory.

30 See chapter two in Alastair Gordon, *Weekend Utopia: Modern Living in the Hamptons* (New York: Princeton Architectural Press, 2001).

31 Sunset *Cabin Plan Book* (San Francisco: Lane Publishing, 1938).

32 "Secrets of a Self-Indulgent Summer: Vacation Shapes," *Living for Young Homemakers*, July 1961, 41.

33 See Alan Hess, *Googie: Fifties Coffee Shop Architecture* (San Francisco: Chronicle, 1985).

34 "Idea Cabin," *Sunset*, May 1958, 80.

35 *Leisure-Time Homes of Fir Plywood* (Tacoma, Wash.: Douglas Fir Plywood Association, 1958), 5.

36 From Kirk Wilkinson to George Matsumoto, 31 July 1960, in the George Matsumoto Papers and Drawings, MC# 42.3, Special Collections Department, North Carolina State University Libraries, Raleigh, N.C.

37 *Builder's Guide to the Second Home Market* (Tacoma, Wash.: Douglas Fir Plywood Association, 1964), 5.

CHAPTER 3

1 Much of the information about the Reemelin A-frames was obtained during a tour given by Reemelin of his houses and an interview with the author, Berkeley, Calif., 22 April 2003.

2 "Chalet on Berkeley Hillside," *Architectural Record*, May 1950, 32–1.

3 Although Reemelin had a degree in civil engineering, his business partner, Charles U. Kring, did the structural calculations for the A-frames.

4 "A Vacation Cabin—The Painless Way," *San Francisco Examiner*, 8 May 1955, sec. 3.

5 Campbell trained at the Rudolph Schaeffer School of Design in San Francisco and during World War II was involved in the development of camouflage techniques for the military. Shortly after the war he set up an office with local architect Worley Wong, whom he had met in the military. The partnership was a convenient arrangement for Campbell, who had no formal training in architecture, and was not licensed (at the time) to practice. Terry Tong, telephone interview by the author, 29 June 2000. Despite the fact that Campbell and Wong shared attribution on all of their published projects, Campbell alone conceived of the Leisure House scheme. This assertion is supported by telephone interviews with Terry Tong, who was an apprentice in the office at the time; Myra Brocchini and Eva Chan, who joined the firm later; and Campbell's partner of thirty-five years, John Seaver. Several magazine articles also list Campbell as the designer. Later, when Campbell and Wong had discontinued their partnership, Campbell remained involved with the Leisure House at his new firm.

6 "Quonset Cabin, Fallen Leaf Lake, California," *Progressive Architecture,* September 1947, 63. Material shortages immediately after the war, combined with the modernist's attraction to the purity of the barrel vault, led several designers to adapt the Quonset hut for nonmilitary functions. In 1945 architect Bruce Goff built a Quonset church at Camp Parks, near Oakland. In 1946 Pierre Chareau designed a Long Island home and studio based on a surplus Quonset for artist Robert Motherwell.

7 "Quonset Cabin," *Progressive Architecture,* 63. The following year the same magazine awarded the design a "Class Two Mention" when it looked back on its series of critiques. *Progressive Architecture,* June 1948, 29.

8 "Holidays in an Equilateral Triangle," *Interiors,* January 1951, 88.

9 "A Small Hill Camp," *Arts and Architecture,* May 1951, 34.

10 "A Leisure House," *Arts and Architecture,* January 1952, 18.

11 "Week-End Cabin for Less Than $500," *San Francisco Chronicle,* 21 October 1951, sec. L, p. 2.

12 Eva Chan (an architect who worked with Campbell and Wong in the late 1950s), telephone interview by the author, 28 June 2000. According to Terry Tong, the Leisure House was never more than a side project for the firm. In fact, Tong recalled that his work on the scheme was not even done on office time. Terry Tong, telephone interview by the author, 29 June 2000.

13 Press release, "The Leisure House," dated 30 July 1954, on Campbell and Wong letterhead, files of the author.

14 Terry Tong, blueprint, House at 71 Greenwood Way, Mill Valley, Calif., for John Carden Campbell's Leisure House, dated 24 February 1952, files of the author. Lawrence Gilmour, the present owner of the much-altered house in Mill Valley, recalls meeting an architect of Chinese ethnicity at a gallery opening in the early 1980s. The architect saw Gilmour filling in the guest book and, recognizing Gilmour's address, remarked that he had helped move a house to that location in the 1950s. He went on to say that the house had originally been built for an art festival in San Francisco. If this statement was true, it is safe to conclude that Campbell built his Mill Valley house with the shell of the Arts Festival model. Lawrence Gilmour, telephone interview by the author, 8 April 2000.

15 In May 1953 Leisure House, Inc. was established with the same address as the Campbell and Wong office. Later that year operation of the company shifted to Los Angeles, where a local businessman was hired to promote and sell Leisure House kits throughout the country, with an original emphasis on California. Eventually a Denver firm called Sheridan and Hanson Productions, which billed itself as the national franchised producers of Leisure House, either took over or supplemented the work done in Los Angeles. The basic Leisure House package featured in the Sheridan and

Hanson brochure is identical to the earlier versions produced in California. It sold for $1,595 (with each additional four-foot extension adding another $199 to the price tag). Perhaps owing to the severe weather and military facilities in the region, the producers noted that because of the equilateral triangle's inherent strength, potential buyers could "discard [their] worries where heavy snow loads, high winds, and near bombings exists." Sheridan and Hansen Productions, Leisure House brochure (Denver: Sheridan and Hansen Productions, n.d.).

16 "Summer Shelters," *Look,* 20 May 1952, 73.

17 "Shakeup at *Look,*" *Time,* 11 January 1954, 50. Quoted in Alan Nourie and Barbara Nourie, eds., *American Mass-Market Magazines* (New York: Greenwood Press, 1990), 230.

18 Kenneth Pratt, "Ideas Make the Difference," *San Francisco Chronicle,* 1 March 1953, sec. L, p. 4.

19 The advertisement for the Vacation Carnival ran beneath an article about Campbell's kit. "A Leisure House for Your Leisure Hours," *San Francisco Chronicle,* 3 May 1953, sec. L, p. 3.

20 William J. Hennessey, *Vacation Houses* (New York: Harper & Brothers, 1962), 54.

21 Campbell's involvement with the Leisure House continued until at least 1971, when the current edition of *Sunset's Cabins and Vacation Houses* directed inquiries to Campbell and Rocchia, the name of Campbell's successor firm. *Cabins and Vacation Houses* (Menlo Park, Calif.: Lane Books, 1971), 82. Myra Brocchini and Terry Tong, who both worked at the Campbell and Wong office throughout the 1950s, felt that the firm never earned much of a profit from the scheme. These recollections suggest that, though Campbell may have sold a lot of plan packages, the precutting and franchising arms of his project were less successful. Perhaps this enterprise appeared too early in the A-frame's popular ascent.

22 David Perlman, telephone interview by the author, 27 January 2002.

23 Ibid.

24 "A Triangular Ski Cabin," in *Cabins and Vacation Houses,* 10.

25 "Uberhangengogel," *Tech Engineering News,* May 1954, 20.

26 Ibid., 22. The sawmill that provided the timber required a year-advance notice to provide a sufficient quantity.

27 Ibid.

28 Henrik Bull, letter to the author, 11 December 2001. The house was featured in *Sunset* magazine in 1958. "Idea Cabin: With Its Unusual Folded Roof…The Feeling of a Mountain Lookout," *Sunset,* May 1958, 80.

29 See Alastair Gordon, *Beach Houses: Andrew Geller* (New York: Princeton Architectural Press, 2003).

30 Andrew Geller, interview by the author, 3 March 2002.

31 Alastair Gordon, *Weekend Utopia: Modern Living in the Hamptons* (New York: Princeton

Architectural Press, 2001), 107.

32 Andrew Geller, interview by the author, 28 June 2003.

33 Fred Smith, "Houses That Unsquare the Cube,"*Sports Illustrated,* 29 July 1963, 40.

CHAPTER 4

1 "A Leisure House for Your Leisure Hours," *San Francisco Chronicle,* 3 May 1953, sec. L, p. 3.

2 USDA, "A-frame Cabin," Cooperative Farm Building Plan Exchange, Plan No. 6003, USDA, Miscellaneous Publication No. 1093, October 1968.

3 Western Wood Products Association, *Vacationland Homes* (Portland, Oreg.: Western Wood Products Association, 1960), 7.

4 Robert C. Broward, telephone interview by the author, 11 September 2003. Blair Barner, telephone interview by the author, 14 August 2003.

5 William Thompson Jr., "Holiday House for Sportsmen," *Field and Stream,* October 1960, 69.

6 Calvin Rutstrum, *The Wilderness Cabin* (New York: Macmillan, 1961), 11. In a later discussion the same book states that "plywood cabins, though classed as frame cabins, are really developing into a new and novel type of their own. The values of this type of construction are its tensile strength, its extreme lightness, and its speedy construction. It can almost be said that with a few dimensional support pieces and a few sheets of plywood, you have material for a cabin."

7 Potlatch Forests and the Home Building Plan Service, *Free-Time Homes,* 2nd ed. (Lewiston, Idaho: Potlatch Forests and the Home Building Plan Service, 1962).

8 Sheldon M. Gallager, "Why the Big Boom in A-frames?" *Popular Science,* August 1961, 128.

9 Douglas Fir Plywood Association, *Leisure-Time Homes of Fir Plywood* (Tacoma, Wash.: Douglas Fir Plywood Association, 1958), 5.

10 *Cabins and Vacation Houses* (Menlo Park, Calif.: Lane Books, 1971), 109.

11 Douglas Fir Plywood Association, *Leisure-Time Homes,* inside cover.

12 Don Jaenicke (former DFPA special projects director), telephone interview by the author, 16 May 2000.

13 The advertisements, titled *Vacation Cabin Ideas,* appeared in the May, July, and September 1958 issues of *Sunset.* According to a DFPA employee, ads also ran in the *Saturday Evening Post* and other magazines. Don Jaenicke, telephone interview by the author, 16 May 2000.

14 Don Jaenicke, letter to Dr. David T. Hellyer, undated.

15 "A Vacation Cabin of Your Own," *Changing Times,* May 1959, 13.

16 Dr. David T. Hellyer, interview by the author, Eatonville, Wash., 24 April 2003. Years later Hellyer recalled that he enjoyed designing and constructing the house more than he did vacationing in it. Over the next twelve years his family visited the A-frame less and less frequently, gradually realizing that they were "not beach people but mountain people." In 1970 they sold it to friends, who still own it more than thirty years later. Hellyer went on to design and build several other modest vacation homes, including two more variations on the A-frame.

17 Douglas Fir Plywood Association, *Leisure-Time Homes*, 5.

18 Ibid.

19 "Adaptable A-frame Popular for Vacation Homes," NAHB *Journal of Homebuilding*, August 1962, 66.

20 *Builder's Guide to the Second Home Market* (Tacoma, Wash.: Douglas Fir Plywood Association, 1964), Appendix, 6. Hellyer's "A-frame Beach Cabin" and Matsumoto's "Low-Cost Dream House" each received fourteen percent of the three hundred thousand inquiries. Henrik Bull's "Convertible Cabin" was next with nine percent.

21 Western Wood Products Association, *Vacationland Homes* (Portland, Oreg.: Western Wood Products Association, 1960), 1.

22 Bob Hunt, personal correspondence to author, 11 January 2000.

23 Bob Hunt, personal correspondence to author, 14 January 2000.

24 Potlatch and HBPS, *Free-Time Homes*.

25 Ibid., 21.

26 Ibid. Lock-Deck was a tongue-and-groove laminated roof, wall, and floor decking that had separate facings on the interior and exterior surfaces. Potlatch claimed that the material could be used alone, without one's resorting to multiple roofing layers. Its strength and rigidity meant that supporting triangular trusses, which were separated by four-foot intervals in typical A-frame designs, could be spaced up to twelve feet apart.

27 "The A-frame: New Models Are Popping Up All Over," *House and Home*, July 1962, 168.

28 "Vacation Cabin Ideas for Editors," undated booklet, American Plywood Association Archives.

CHAPTER 5

1 "The Pre-Cut or Pre-Fab Cabin...Bargain or Not?" *Sunset*, July 1958, 76.

2 Although the history of precutting structures goes back centuries, postwar precut A-frames had their roots in the late-nineteenth-century "mail-order houses" like Sears, Roebuck, & Co. and the Aladdin Company, among others. Burnham Kelly, *The Prefabrication of Houses* (Cambridge, Mass.: MIT Press, 1951), 11.

3 "How to Tap the Vacation Cottages Market," *Building Supply News*, June 1962, 72–73.

4 Lester David, "The Truth About Prefabs," *Mechanix Illustrated*, June 1968, 98.

5 Picking up the package at the lumberyard saved considerable shipping charges. A 1953 article in the *San Francisco Chronicle* noted that "if you have a trailer you can pick up the Leisure House package in San Francisco and haul it away

yourself. The unit weighs 5,600 pounds and the number of trips would depend upon the size and strength of your trailer. A small rented truck would do the job nicely." "A Leisure House for Your Leisure Hours," *San Francisco Chronicle*, 3 May 1953, sec. L, p. 3.

6 Lindal Cedar Homes, plan book (Tacoma, Wash.: Lindal Cedar Homes, 1969), 2. According to Sir Walter Lindal, he is not a knight. His first name is an English translation of his Icelandic birth name "Spuli," a name shared by noble relations in Iceland.

7 "Roof Structure," Patent No. 3,378,966, by Spuli Walter Lindal, filed 22 October 1965.

8 "Holiday House Built for Fun," *Popular Mechanics*, April 1966.

9 Sir Walter Lindal, interview by the author, Seattle, Wash., 25 April 2003.

10 Sir Walter Lindal, telephone interview by the author, 3 July 2000.

11 Prior to World War II, prefabrication was largely limited to low-volume experimentation. It took the war and its demand for quick, cheap, and portable housing to set the stage for the concept's significant postwar growth. In 1947, approximately thirty-seven thousand new homes were built with prefabricated components. Thirteen years later the number had increased to 126,000, or nine percent of the total homes constructed. Throughout the postwar period, the growing application of prefab techniques to permanent-house construction (of Lustron and TechBuilt homes, for example) was paralleled by the growth of prefab units aimed at the booming vacation home market. See A. M. Watkins, *Building or Buying the High Quality House at Lowest Cost* (Garden City, N.Y.: Dolphin/Doubleday, 1962), 172; and Kelly, *Prefabrication of Houses*.

12 Structural sandwich panels were also referred to as "stressed skin panels." These components derived their strength from the apportioning of forces between the stringers and the plywood or metal faces. Stringers functioned as built-up I-beams, which took sheer force, while the skins took moment stresses and acted as interior and exterior sheathing. The use of stressed skin panels grew out of experiments sponsored by builders, wood associations, and federal agencies throughout the first half of the twentieth century. Foster Gunnison's company, Gunnison Magic Homes, was the first to produce year-round homes with stressed skin plywood panels. See Douglas Fir Plywood Association, *DFPA Specification No. SS-8, Stressed Skin Panels* (Tacoma, Wash.: Douglas Fir Plywood Association, 1963), 1; and Kelly, *Prefabrications of Houses*, 77.

13 "Modern Engineering Can Help You," *Manufactured Homes*, July 1960, 8.

14 Bart M. Jacob, telephone interview by the author, 3 March 2000.

15 Ibid.

16 "Patent Pending Prompts Prefab Builders to Revise Their Plans," *Brattleboro Daily Reformer*, 30 October 1962, special section.

17 "A for Adaptable," *Time*, 8 December 1961, 56.

18 "Prefab Panel Patent Is New Concept in A-frames," *Brattleboro Daily Reformer*, 30 October 1962, special section.

19 "A-Frame Construction," Patent No. 3,177,618, by Bart M. Jacob, filed June 4, 1962.

20 "Prefab Panel Patent," photo caption. Using the panels and their structural beams on all three sides, Jacob's design formed an equilateral-triangle truss.

21 "The Alpan Home," unpublished brochure, Alpine Villages, Wilmington, Vt., n.d.

22 "Patent Pending," *Brattleboro Daily Reformer*, 30 October 1962. Four years earlier, Koppers had manufactured similar panels for an experimental A-frame carport. See "Conclusion."

23 "The Alpan Home." The company also established relationships with local builders, who would finish the interior spaces, became familiar with the packages, and functioned essentially as dealers.

24 Bart M. Jacob, telephone interview by the author, 3 March 2000.

25 Other manufacturers known to have produced prefabricated A-frame kits include Holiday House Manufacturing Corporation, in Fort Worth, Texas; Ernest Pierson Company, in Eureka, California; Boise-Cascade, of Boise, Idaho; and Swift Homes, in Elizabeth, Pennsylvania. In some cases the A-frame was the only model offered; in others it was one of a number of vacation home kits.

26 Sheldon M. Gallager, "Why the Big Boom in A-frames?" *Popular Science*, August 1961, 130.

27 Burt Zusman (former president of Leisure Homes), telephone interview by the author, 16 May 2000. Also see "Cashing In on the Second-Home Market," *Automation in Housing*, April 1966, 72.

28 David, "Truth About Prefabs," 72. According to Philip Langdon, many of the A-frame restaurants that appeared in the 1960s were built using Reynolds's wall panels and roof shingles. Philip Langdon, *Orange Roofs, Golden Arches* (New York: Knopf, 1986), 96. "Plastics Ski Lodge," *Plastics World*, February 1963, 38.

29 Corwin Hockett, Reynolds's project development engineer, quoted in Jim Rutherford, "New Ideas in Prefab Cabins," *Field and Stream*, June 1966, 65.

30 "A-frame House Prefabricated," *New York Times*, 22 September 1968, sec. 8R. Also see Rutherford, "New Ideas," 64.

31 "Leisure Home Specialist," *Building Materials Merchandiser*, May 1963, 110.

32 "Ski Expansion Slows," *Ski*, 20 November 1966.

33 Downhill skiing also benefited from developments in equipment (metal and then fiberglass skis, plastic boots), as well as lift and mechanical-grooming technology. The widespread adoption of chairlifts and gondolas was probably the single most important factor in the growth of downhill skiing as a sport and ski resorts as vacation destinations. In 1956 there were less than eighty steel-cable uphill lifts in North America. Ten years later that number had grown to more than 680. "Ski Expansion Slows."

34 Hellyer wrote about his work with Ski Lifts, Incorporated in his memoir, *At the Forest's Edge* (Seattle: University of Washington Press, 1985), 184. Ski historian Kirby Gilbert provided additional information about the hut, telephone interview by the author, 17 August 2003.

35 Squaw Valley Ski Corporation, *Squaw Valley USA: The First Fifty Years*, brochure (Olympic Valley, Calif.: Squaw Valley Ski Corporation, 1999).

36 J. E. Carpenter, *California Winter Sports and the VIII Winter Olympic Games at Squaw Valley* (San Francisco: Fearon Publishers, 1958): 17. Both buildings remain at Squaw Valley, their exteriors largely unaltered. The old Nevada center now houses a rental shop, bathrooms, a general store, the Red Dog Saloon, and offices. The California building is a members locker room.

37 Donald Miller, "Vacation Homes for Ski Areas," *Ski Area Management*, Winter 1963, 27.

38 The Alfred A. Braun Hut System, near Aspen, Colorado, also featured an A-frame. Tagert Hut was built in 1964 on the site of a former dam tender's cabin, which backcountry hikers and skiers had long used as a shelter. With scalloped eaves and small windows, the A-frame was a typical Alpine-themed triangular shelter, well suited to its role as an isolated mountain refuge. In 1999 it was fully renovated. See John Fry, "The High Huts," *Ski*, March, 1965, 54; and Tenth Mountain Division Hut Association, "Tagert and Green Wilson Huts," http://www.huts.org/hut_details/tagert_green_hut_details.html (accessed October 31, 2002). Ned Robinson, letter to author, 13 July 2002. Robinson directed the construction of both Sierra Club A-frames in the 1950s. Information on the Sierra Huts was also provided by Richard Simpson.

39 United States Forest Service, Wrangell Ranger District, unpublished history of the cabins at Tongass National Forest, n.d.

40 United States Department of Agriculture, *A-Frame Cabins. Plan Nos. 5964, 5965* (Washington, D.C.: USDA Cooperative Farm Building Plan Exchange, 1964); and *A-frame Cabin. Plan No. 6003* (Washington, D.C.: USDA Cooperative Farm Building Plan Exchange, 1968).

41 "A for Adaptable," 56.

42 "Haus Wenger (das Trigon)," *Schweizer Architecktur*, March 1998, 128–31; *Schweizer Architekturfuhrer 1920–1990*, bd. 3; "Mount Pleasant," *Wallpaper*, March 2002, 173; Heidi and Peter Wenger, *Leibensraume—Spielraume* (Basel: self-published, 1980).

43 Heidi and Peter Wenger, letter to the author, 14 July 2003.

44 Per Hederus, letter to the author, 9 June 2003. Per Hederus is the son of Folke Hederus.

45 "I Stallet For Talt Och Ladstugor," *Villa Tidskriften Hem i Svenge*, 3 April 1959, 91. The issue was devoted to summer homes and featured the Wengers' Trigon and an earlier vacation home by Folke Hederus.

46 "Art of Young Architects: Igor Vasilevsky," *Architecture of the Soviet Union*, November, 1968, 40. Triangular, A-frame-like buildings are called *dom shalash* (roof houses) in Russian. They have traditionally been used as temporary shelters, built, for example, when loggers were working far from their homes. According to Elena Hazelwood, a native of Moscow, Russians are familiar with the story that, immediately before the 1917 revolution, Lenin hid for three nights from the czar's police in a *shalash* outside St. Petersburg.

47 "The Kusazaki Club," *Japan Architect*, September 1964, 33; and "A Hexagonal Mountain Lodge," *Japan Architect*, March 1966, 61.

48 "A Mountain Lodge with a Principal Rafter," *Japan Architect*, August 1964, 55.

CHAPTER 6

1 For a discussion of the various motel forms, see "The Motel as Architecture," *The Motel in America*, by John A. Jakle et al., (Baltimore: Johns Hopkins University Press, 1996).

2 "How to Tap the Vacation Cottages Market," *Building Supply News*, June 1962, 72–73.

3 Karen Bowman, telephone interview by the author, 2 June 2003.

4 Jakle, *Motel in America*, 187.

5 The history of Harmon Dobson and the Whataburger chain can be found in Greg Woolridge's commemorative book, *Whataburger: The Tale of a Texas Icon 1950–2000* (Corpus Christi, Tex.: Whataburger, 2000). Additional information was provided by Dobson's son Hugh; telephone interview by the author, 9 January 2003.

6 Jakle and his co-authors, Keith Sculle and Jefferson Rogers, discuss the intersection of commercial architecture, logos, and signage in their books: Jackle, Sculle, and Rogers, *Motel in America*; John A. Jakle and Keith A. Sculle, *The Gas Station in America* (Baltimore: Johns Hopkins University Press, 1994); John A. Jakle and Keith A. Sculle, *Fast Food: Roadside Restaurants in the Automobile Age* (Baltimore: Johns Hopkins University Press, 1999).

7 Woolridge, *Whataburger*, 83.

8 Quoted in Woolridge, *Whataburger*, 99.

9 Tom Amberger, director of marketing for the Galardi Group, letter to the author, 29 April 2003.

10 Quoted in Philip Langdon, *Orange Roofs, Golden Arches: The Architecture of American Chain Restaurants* (New York: Knopf, 1986), 97.

11 Robert Venturi, Denise Scott Brown, Steven

Izenour, *Learning from Las Vegas* (Cambridge, Mass.: MIT Press, 1972).

12 George Cline Smith, "Seventy-Thousand Churches in Ten Years," *Architectural Record*, June 1955.

13 Katherine Morrison McClinton, *The Changing Church: Its Architecture, Art and Decoration* (New York: Morehouse-Gorham, 1957), 13. Also see Pietro Belluschi, "The Churches Go Modern," *Saturday Evening Post*, 4 October 1958, 36.

14 Many critics found the variety overwhelming and unfortunate. See "Anarchy in Our Churches," *Architectural Forum*, December 1952, 93.

15 John W. Ragsdale, "We Will Build Modern Churches," *Architectural Record*, October 1946, 97.

16 Though commonly referred to as "A-frame churches," the buildings that followed were rarely structural A-frames. Even those constructed of wood did not incorporate the cross-tie common among triangular vacation homes.

17 The Unitarian Meeting House was one of several religious designs that Wright undertook during the postwar era. Each was a completely distinct expression, based on the programmatic and symbolic needs of the congregation for which it was developed. His 1958 Pilgrim Congregational Church, in Redding, California, was originally based on an equilateral triangle, though, in its final form, a pitched roof was suspended from concrete bents, resulting in a gambrel-like shape.

18 Quoted in Yukio Futagawa and Bruce Brooks Pfeiffer, eds., *Frank Lloyd Wright: Preliminary Studies 1933–59* (Tokyo: A.D.A. Edita, 1987), 158.

19 Reverend Kenneth J. Gerike (current pastor of Trinity Lutheran Church), letter to the author, 8 October 2002. Bruce Brooks Pfeiffer, in *Frank Lloyd Wright: Preliminary Studies 1933–59* writes that the Unitarian Meeting House roof was described by Wright's third wife, Olgivanna Milanoff, as "like the hands together in the attitude of prayer."

20 Michael Sheppard (former Creative Buildings, Incorporated employee), telephone interview by the author, 20 June 2002. The Small Homes Council, a University of Illinois construction research institute that was involved in integrating modern manufacturing processes with home construction, was also based in Urbana.

21 "New Church Design Shows Versatility of Precast, Prestressed Concrete," advertisement for Lehigh Portland Cement Company, *Progressive Architecture*, October 1958, 265.

22 Reverend Eugenia M. Durham, letter to the author, 15 September 2002.

23 Concurrent to the Concordia project, Saarinen was working on the Kresge Auditorium and chapel at the Massachusetts Institute of Technology, in Boston. Though the shape of his cylindrical brick chapel at MIT differed from that developed for Concordia, it exhibited a similar geometric purity, concern with material texture, and reliance on a creative natural-lighting scheme. The college is now called Concordia Theological Seminary. The chapel is known as Kramer Chapel.

24 "A Village Design for a College Campus," *Progressive Architecture*, December 1958, 89. In the article Saarinen states that the pitched roof was "symbolic of the North European church."

25 The diamond-shaped Concordia bricks were identical to those used in the walls of the dormitories and other campus buildings. In the chapel they pointed vertically, according to the Reverend Professor Robert V. Roethemeyer, to suggest "a conversation between God and man—God's gifts are sent down and man's thanks and praise are directed upwards." Roethemeyer noted that in the other buildings, the bricks were oriented horizontally to reflect a sense of community. Reverend Professor Robert V. Roethemeyer (assistant professor of pastoral ministry and missions and director of library and information services, Concordia Theological Seminary), interview by the author, Fort Wayne, Ind., 26 July 2002.

26 Commission on Church Architecture of the Lutheran Church, *Architecture and the Church* (St. Louis: Missouri Synod, 1965), 96.

27 Aline B. Saarinen, ed., *Eero Saarinen on His Work* (New Haven, Conn.: Yale University Press, 1968), 44.

28 Roethemeyer, interview

29 Albert Christ-Janer and Mary Mix Foley, *Modern Church Architecture: A Guide to the Form and Spirit of 20th Century Religious Buildings* (New York: Dodge Book Dept., McGraw-Hill, 1962), 311.

30 Taffel, who apprenticed to Frank Lloyd Wright, designed an A-frame variation whose sides did not meet at the structure's apex and did not reach the ground. Rather than joining at the peak, the roof planes appeared to hang on the structural framework. "Airport Chapels Are Among Award-Winning Queens Buildings," *New York Times*, 4 December 1966, sec. 8.

31 Netsch's scheme originally met with fierce resistance, which led Congress to temporarily freeze the funding for the entire Academy project. When plans for the structure were reviewed by a Senate delegation, one legislator likened the chapel to an "assembly of wigwams," while another called it an "insult to God." Nathaniel Ownings, *The Spaces in Between: An Architect's Journey* (Boston: Houghton/Mifflin, 1973), 157.

32 Architects E. Eerikainen and O. Sipari designed a triangular church in the late 1940s that was built in the Finnish village of Salla. It would be interesting to learn if Eero Saarinen had ever seen the building since it is similar in many ways to his Kramer Chapel at the Concordia Theological Seminary.

33 Helge Abrahamsen, "Norsk Kirkearkitektur Etter Krigen," in Fin Jor, ed. *Kirker i en ny tid* (Oslo: Land og Kirke, 1966), 53.

34 Ibid., 64.

35 Information about the Unification Church A-frames was provided by the Church administrator, Julian Gray. Julian Gray, letter to the author, 25 March 2003.

36 John Knox Shear, "On Getting Good Architecture for the Church," in *Religious Buildings for Today*, ed. John Knox Shear (New York: F.W. Dodge, 1957), 6.

37 Alvin L. Rubin, "Would You Build Another Contemporary Church?" *Architectural Record*, December 1954, 148.

CHAPTER 7

1 "Vacation Homes: An Exploding Market Takes on a New Shape," *House & Home*, February 1964, 111.

2 Former Swift Homes president Ira Gordon estimated that, before the company went out of business in the early 1980s, it sold between 350,000 and 400,000 homes. A network of dealers extended its range across twenty-eight states and into Britain and Europe. From an interview in *Houses Around Here*, producer and writer Rick Sebak, 60 min., QED Communications, 1994, videocassette.

3 Francis Bannon (former Swift employee), telephone interview by the author, 31 March 2000.

4 Bannon recalled that after some initial difficulties with a union that was resentful that Swift's crew erected the model, the structure remained in the dissonant, though heavily trafficked, location for three months. Bannon interview.

5 Another example of the overlap of A-frames and permanent home sales is the group of New England developers who, in 1964, established a fifty-acre subdivision intended for year-round living near New Haven, Connecticut. Customers were expected to buy a lakefront lot and arrange for the construction of a permanent home, the design of which was subject to approval by the developers. In order to establish the "character of the development" and to attract prospective residents, the developers hired a local builder to erect a 1,900-square-foot cross-gable A-frame as a model home. Builder J. Forest Ventner said that "the model is so striking, both in form and its use of natural wood, that we have been pulling greater crowds than we can handle." "Double A-frame Draws Crowds to a Custom-House Subdivision," *House & Home*, February 1964, 45.

6 *National Association of Home Builders Research House, South Bend, Indiana, 1958: A Summary Report* (Washington, D.C.: National Association of Home Builders, 1958), 39.

7 The first A-frame shown at such an event was probably John Campbell's Leisure House. It was exhibited at the 1951 San Francisco Arts Festival, five months later at the San Francisco Boat, Travel, and Sports Show, and the following year at the Roos Brothers department store's Vacation Carnival.

8 Title illegible, *Boston Herald*, 21 April 1960, no page number.

9 Hellyer maintained a scrapbook of several newspaper clippings and personal letters regarding the A-frame. It includes a letter to the *Boston Herald*, written by Ralph Gould in April 1960. In response to the misattribution of the A-frame, Gould wrote, "I believe that this cabin was designed by Dr. David T. Hellyer of Tacoma, Washington, not the good Frank Lloyd Wright. Out of courtesy to Dr. Hellyer and the late Frank Lloyd Wright I believe that this misstatement should be corrected. The reason I am aware of the designer is that I built one of these cabins with a cellar as a ski lodge in Bridgton, Maine." Correspondence, Ralph Gould to the *Boston Herald*, 19 April 1960, private collection of David Hellyer.

10 The ad for the show ran in the *Washington Post*, 17 February 1961.

11 "Pittsburgh Paints $100,000 Sweepstakes," advertisement, *Better Homes and Gardens*, June 1962, 41.

12 "Libby's 'Cabin in the Mountains' Sweepstakes," advertisement, *Sunset*, May 1965.

13 Building Products' Guide to Vacation and Leisure Homes (Los Angeles: Hudson Publishers, 1968).

14 A-frame imagery was also used to encourage the sale of recreation land. A 1960 advertisement in *Sunset* for a vacation home development called Pla-Vada Woodlands, near Lake Tahoe, featured an image of a cozy A-frame at the base of a mountain, hidden among the pine trees, a wisp of smoke rising from the chimney. At the close of the decade, Reforestation, Incorporated, which sold cutover timberland for use as vacation home lots, placed a similar ad in *Outdoor Life*. Again the A-frame was nestled among pine trees, the mountain in the distance mirroring the steeply pitched roof. "Land!" advertisement, *Outdoor Life*, July 1970, 125.

15 "Carefree Tent-House," *House and Garden*, June 1958, 79.

16 "Johnson. Ask the Man Who Knows the Territory," advertisement, *Field & Stream*, December 1967, 29.

17 "Yamaha. Start Something New!" advertisement, *Playboy*, September 1967, 263.

18 Malcolm B. VerNooy, telephone interview by the author, 27 October 2002.

19 Ibid.

20 Untitled press release by Rene A. Henry Jr., issued by Lennen & Newell News Bureau, San Francisco, mailed 29 November 1963.

21 "A Wonderful A-frame Playhouse," *Science and Mechanics*, August 1964, 76.

22 "Build a Modern Tree House—With or Without a Tree," *Popular Mechanics*, June 1965, 126.

23 Ralph S. Wilkes, "How You Can Build an A-frame Playhouse," *Popular Science*, July 1965, 124.

24 "A Is for A-frame—And a Lot of Fun," *Better Homes and Gardens*, May 1966; "Starting with an Old Gym Set Frame…He Built This Cheerful Playhouse," *Sunset*, August 1966, 58; "100 Ideas for Under $100: A-frame for Small Fry," *Better Homes and Gardens*, July 1967, 40.

25 "Redwood A-frame You Can Build," *Mechanix Illustrated*, September 1965, 70.

26 Photographs of the house, taken by Giovanni Suter, are part of the Hedrich-Blessing photograph collection at the Chicago Historical Society. Notes indicate that they were published in *Better Homes and Gardens* in 1962.

27 William Daniels (son of Carroll Daniels), telephone interview by the author, 7 June 2003.

28 "You'll Find Fascinating Ideas at Your Weyerhaeuser 4-Square Lumber Dealer," advertisement, *Better Homes and Gardens*, May 1960.

29 "Garden Accents," *Home Maintenance and Improvement* 16:2 (1965): 4.

30 "The Dog Likes It Fine," *Sunset*, April 1959, 272; and "Under Reed and Plastic: An Orchid Collection," *Sunset*, November 1959, 208.

31 See, for example, plans for a dollhouse in a Rochester, New York, newspaper. Bill Meyerriecks, "Easy, Inexpensive Doll Houses," *Democrat and Chronicle*, 3 November 1963, sec. H, p. 4.

32 Deanna Korth (director of the Toy Town Museum), letter to the author, 26 January 2000. The Toy Town Museum is based in the same town as Fisher-Price, in East Aurora, New York.

33 One actually did. See the A-frame designed for Johnson Motors discussed earlier in this chapter.

34 A sign that the triangular dollhouse is not dead, German toy manufacturer Playmobil released an A-frame Family Vacation Home in the United States in the spring of 2003.

35 Richard B. Pollman, *151 Vacation Houses* (New York: Grosset & Dunlap, 1968), 21.

CONCLUSION

1 "Away from It All: The Second Home Boom," *Newsweek*, 5 August 1968, 58.

2 "A Market for Relaxation Stirs a Hive of Activity," *Business Week*, 19 July 1969, 66. Also see "The Corporate Land Rush of 1970," *Business Week*, 29 August 1970, 72.

3 Glenn Fowler, "For Rent Signs Found at Resorts," *New York Times*, 5 July 1970, sec. 8.

4 "For 'Second Home' Owners: A Stiff New Tax Rule," *U.S. News and World Report*, 24 July 1972, 63. Throughout the previous decade, vacation-home owners who rented their structures for part of the year were able to deduct the operating "loss" from their ordinary income. New regulations, established in the summer of 1972, closed this loophole. Thenceforth only owners who used their vacation homes solely for rental income were able to take a deduction. See also "Second Thoughts on 'Second Homes,'" *U.S. News and World Report*, 26 August 1974, 76.

5 Saddled with empty lots surrounding expensive golf courses and marinas, investors like Boise Cascade moved quickly to unload prefab enterprises, land holdings, and resort communities from their portfolios. "Idaho's Cold Potato," *Newsweek*, 13 March 1972, 82. See also "Boise Cascade Shifts Toward Tighter Control," *Business Week*, 15 May 1971, 86.

6 Some were able to see the silver lining. Distressed selling by developers offered the chance to obtain a cheap vacation home, especially one located more than a hundred miles from population centers. See Frank K. Coffee, "Big Bargains in Vacation Homes," *Mechanix Illustrated*, June 1974, 90.

7 "Market for Relaxation," *Business Week*, 66.

8 Bob Cram, "Ski Life," *Ski*, September 1968, 75.

9 Telephone interview with an Adirondacks real estate agent, June 5, 2003.

10 See chapter one for a discussion of Teapot Hall.

11 Rex Roberts, *Your Engineered House* (New York: M. Evans & Co., 1964), 53.

12 Alan Liddle, "Whither Alpine Architecture in America?" *Ski*, December 1964, 8.

13 Ibid.

14 Ironically, such roofs were less amenable to dormers and inset vertical walls and thus were often darker than variations that retained the triangular shape.

15 Chuck Crandall, *They Chose to Be Different: Unusual California Homes* (San Francisco: Chronicle, 1972), foreword.

16 "Five Great Vacation Homes," *Popular Mechanics*, May 1973, 85.

17 "New Sparkle in the Vacation Home Market" *American Builder*, July 196, 63.

18 Mark Wingfield, "What About a Church at a Whataburger?" *Baptist Standard: The News Journal of Texas Baptists* 3:3 (4 August 1999): 1.

19 Betsy Schiffman, "Ski House Buyer's Guide 2003," *Forbes*, 20 December 2002.

20 Tracie Rozhon, "Suddenly, One House Isn't Enough," *New York Times*, 8 August 2002, Home and Garden Section.

21 Recent articles discussing the renovation of specific A-frame vacation homes include Jeannie Matteucci, "The Great Escape: A Couple Turn Their Wine Country Getaway into a Year-Round Home," *San Francisco Chronicle*, 3 November 1999, Home and Garden section; and "Take the A-frame," *Metropolitan Home*, July–August 1993, 62.

22 Tony Russomanno, telephone interview by the author, 25 June 2003. Well known at the time for constructing extremely affordable vacation homes, Hack built A-frames and other styles throughout the Tahoe region.

23 "Acadia Summer Arts Program," press release, Venturi, Scott Brown and Associates, 1998.

24 Nan Lincoln, "A Is for Art," *Bar Harbor Times*, 10 September 1998, sec. D, p. 3.

25 Available from http://www.ubild.com/woodworking-projects/381-htm, accessed 31 May 2003. Kevin Taylor, letter to the author, 26 February 2003. Other familiar designs can be found on the HomeStyles website. The successor to the Home Building Plan Service, which was responsible for many of the plan books published in cooperation with Potlatch and other building-material producers, HomeStyles still offers at least five different A-frame plans on its website. Models such as the Avant-Garde A-frame and the True A-frame carry on the tradition and provide the chance for a new generation to build and live in a triangular vacation home. Available from http://www.homestyles.com, accessed 23 November 2003.

205

vacation
every
weekend!